Arab Criminology

The objective of *Arab Criminology* is to establish a criminological subfield called 'Arab Criminology.' The ever-evolving field of criminology has advanced in the past decade, yet many impediments remain. Unlike criminology in Africa, Asia, the Americas, Europe, and Oceania, which is based merely on geopolitical constructs, the Arab world has unique commonalities that do not exist in the other established subfields of criminology. The Arab world has largely remained in criminology's periphery despite the region's considerable importance to current international affairs. In response, this book explores two main questions: Why should we and how do we establish a subfield in Arab criminology? The authors examine the state of criminology in the Arab world, define its parameters, and present four components that bond and distinguish Arab criminology from other criminological area studies. They then identify the requirements for establishing Arab criminology and detail how local, regional, and international researchers can collaborate, develop, and expand the subfield. Arab criminology will challenge some of the recurrent Orientalist and Islamophobic tropes in Northern criminology and progress the discipline of criminology to reflect a more diverse focus that embraces regions from the Global South.

Presenting compelling arguments and examples that support the establishment of this subfield, *Arab Criminology* will be of great interest to scholars of criminology, criminal justice, legal studies, and Middle Eastern/North African studies, particularly those working on Southern criminology, comparative criminology, international criminal justice systems, and Arab studies.

Nabil Ouassini is Assistant Professor at Prairie View A & M University. He received his Ph.D. in criminal justice from Indiana University at Bloomington, and his research interests include comparative criminal justice/criminology, criminal justice reform, legitimation and legitimacy, and crime/criminal justice in the Arab world.

Anwar Ouassini is Associate Professor of Sociology and Criminal Justice at Delaware State University. He received his Ph.D. in sociology from the University of New Mexico, and his research interests include civil society and criminal justice reform in North and West Africa, Arab criminology, and culture/racialization with focus on Muslim minorities.

Criminology in Focus
Series Editor: Sandra Walklate

This series offers a space for a 'short format' book series which showcases and puts the spotlight on new research in criminology. We are interested in books that fit the 'short-form' model; for example: theoretical think pieces, developments in criminal justice policy, paradigm shifting innovations in the fields, a compelling case study that would be of interest to an international readership. We would like to attract 'big names' as well as up-and-coming scholars; all books should speak and contribute to international criminological debates and conversations.

1. **Decolonising Justice for Aboriginal Youth with Foetal Alcohol Spectrum Disorders**
   Tamara Tulich, Harry Blagg, Maewyn Mutch, Robyn Williams, Suzie May and Michelle Stewart

2. **Coercive Control**
   Charlotte Barlow and Sandra Walklate

3. **Applied Photovoice in Criminal Justice**
   Wendy Fitzgibbon

4. **Co-production and Criminal Justice**
   Diana Johns, Catherine Flynn, Maggie Hall, Claire Spivakovsky and Shelley Turner

5. **Arab Criminology**
   Nabil Ouassini and Anwar Ouassini

Arab Criminology

Nabil Ouassini and Anwar Ouassini

LONDON AND NEW YORK

First published 2023
by Routledge
4 Park Square, Milton Park, Abingdon, Oxon OX14 4RN

and by Routledge
605 Third Avenue, New York, NY 10158

Routledge is an imprint of the Taylor & Francis Group, an informa business

© 2023 Nabil Ouassini and Anwar Ouassini

The right of Nabil Ouassini and Anwar Ouassini to be identified as authors of this work has been asserted in accordance with sections 77 and 78 of the Copyright, Designs and Patents Act 1988.

All rights reserved. No part of this book may be reprinted or reproduced or utilised in any form or by any electronic, mechanical, or other means, now known or hereafter invented, including photocopying and recording, or in any information storage or retrieval system, without permission in writing from the publishers.

Trademark notice: Product or corporate names may be trademarks or registered trademarks, and are used only for identification and explanation without intent to infringe.

British Library Cataloguing-in-Publication Data
A catalogue record for this book is available from the British Library

Library of Congress Cataloging-in-Publication Data
Names: Ouassini, Nabil, author. | Ouassini, Anwar, author.
Title: Arab criminology/Nabil Ouassini and Anwar Ouassini.
Description: Abingdon, Oxon; New York, NY: Routledge, 2023. | Series: Criminology in focus | Includes bibliographical references and index. |
Identifiers: LCCN 2022056502 (print) | LCCN 2022056503 (ebook) | ISBN 9780367770990 (hardback) | ISBN 9780367771003 (paperback) | ISBN 9781003169789 (ebook)
Subjects: LCSH: Criminology—Arab countries.
Classification: LCC HV7134. O93 2023 (print) | LCC HV7134 (ebook) | DDC 364.917/4927—dc23/eng/20221129
LC record available at https://lccn.loc.gov/2022056502
LC ebook record available at https://lccn.loc.gov/2022056503

ISBN: 978-0-367-77099-0 (hbk)
ISBN: 978-0-367-77100-3 (pbk)
ISBN: 978-1-003-16978-9 (ebk)

DOI: 10.4324/9781003169789

Typeset in Times New Roman
by Apex CoVantage, LLC

Dedicated to our dear parents:
Abdelmajid and Faouzia Ouassini

Contents

1 Why Arab Criminology? 1

2 The Islamic Legal Tradition 19

3 Historical, Political, and Cultural Commonalities 33

4 Arab Criminology at the Intersection of Race and Gender 49

5 Transnational Crime in the Arab World 68

6 Moving Forward 81

Index 94

1 Why Arab Criminology?

Introduction

The Arab Spring has confounded governments, policy institutions, and scholars in their inability to determine how the historical events transpired without foreseeing the upheaval (Gause, 2011; Bayat, 2013). The first demonstrations occurred at the end of 2010 in Sidi Bouzid, a scruffy rural town with a population of around 40,000 located in the arid Tunisian plains, 160 miles south of the capital Tunis. Residents poured into the streets by the thousands to protest the humiliation and denigration suffered by Mohamed Bouazizi, a 26-year-old fruit vendor. The story of supercilious police officers and their systematic abuses, injustice, and repeated exploitation of residents was familiar to many. The officers often considered the local marketplace as their personal property. Those who refused to recognize that reality were subject to fines, the confiscation of their equipment, and other indignities. On December 17, Bouazizi pushed his cart to the primary market in Sidi Bouzid to sell the fruits he had previously bought on credit, only to face the usual harassment from a 45-year-old female officer Faida Hamdy. The officer had extorted a fruit box, and when she came back for a second box, Bouazizi objected. Officer Hamdy had Bouazizi's fruits and weight scale forcibly confiscated for his defiance. When he pleaded for his merchandise, the officer further humiliated Bouazizi by slapping him in front of the crowd gathered to watch the commotion. Bouazizi demanded his property from the officers in the local municipality, where he was cruelly beaten and, after visiting the governor's office, was denied access to any government officials. Immediately after these encounters, Bouazizi walked to a nearby gas station, filled a container with gasoline, and returned to set himself on fire in front of the governor's office. This incident sparked the eventual resignation and overthrow of several leaders and continual uprisings in multiple Arab countries.

Bouazizi's self-immolation was not directed explicitly against President Ben Ali's authoritarian regime, and there is no preceding evidence to

DOI: 10.4324/9781003169789-1

2 Why Arab Criminology?

indicate that Bouazizi was suicidal or clinically depressed. There is also no support that Bouazizi had a religious motivation or aspired to be a martyr. Bouazizi's act of symbolic violence was an expressive consequence of despair due to the years of arbitrary oppression, unfair treatment, and the criminal justice system's failures that are, unfortunately, standard practices throughout the Arab world. Many citizens in the region are driven to anguish by the abuses from the criminal justice system. Countless others are subjected to torture and oppression by the police and correctional officers, impelling them to suicide and extremism as an outlet for antagonism toward the regimes and criminal justice systems.

Political scientists, economists, anthropologists, sociologists, and other academics have since studied, commented on, and published about the region's conditions pre- and post-Arab Spring with little to no effort from criminologists despite criminal injustice brewing at the forefront of the region's protests (Ouassini & Ouassini, 2020). Bouazizi's ordeal with the criminal justice system resonated in the Arab world as citizens empathized with his affliction and subsequent immolation. Six months prior, Khaled Saeed was beaten to death by Egyptian police in Alexandria (Human Rights Watch, 2010). Pictures displaying Saeed's tortured and disfigured corpse spread through social media as Wael Ghonim and other internet activists created and moderated the Facebook group "We are all Khaled Saeed" that eventually inspired and contributed to Egypt's January 25 Revolution. In Syria, the arrests, detention, abuse, and torture of 15 children in Dara'a for merely scribbling anti-government graffiti on walls incited the ceaseless civil war. Security forces repeatedly opened fire on the detained youth's family and friends, who protested for their release. The regime's intolerance for protests was displayed to the world when Syrian forces delivered the mutilated body of 13-year-old Hamza Ali Al-Khateeb to his family with broken bones, burns, gunshots, and severed genitals (Human Rights Watch, 2011; Stack, 2011). Meanwhile, in Libya, the arrest of Fathi Terbil, a lawyer and human rights advocate, triggered protests in Benghazi. Terbil was one of the few lawyers who willingly represented family members of more than a thousand prisoners massacred in the Abu Salim prison. The maximum-security prison was infamous for housing Qaddafi's political prisoners. Finally, Tawakkol Karman was constantly harassed by plain-clothed officers and imprisoned by the Saleh regime for advocating press freedom, democracy, and human rights in Yemen. Her activism for justice earned her the nickname "the Mother of the Revolution" and the 2011 Nobel Peace Prize. As the face of every regime, the criminal justice system was one of the focal legitimacy issues surrounding the Arab Spring protests. Unfortunately, academic criminological work has been deficient in a region requiring meticulous criminal justice study.

This deficiency is particularly evident in the aftermath of September 11 and the ensuing $6 trillion War on Terror (Crawford, 2019). Terrorism literature has examined political, psychological, ideological, religious, sociological, and economic factors (Crenshaw, 1981; Bjørgo, 2004; Krieger & Meierrieks, 2011; Bjørgo & Silke, 2018; Irfan et al., 2020) but has only recently gained the attention of criminologists (LaFree & Dugan, 2015; LaFree & Freilich, 2016). Criminologists should be at the forefront of the global War on Terror. The region's reactionary criminal justice systems have a reputation of brutal repression as a former CIA agent acknowledged in 2004:

> If you want a serious interrogation, you send a prisoner to Jordan. If you want them to be tortured, you send them to Syria. If you want someone to disappear – never to see them again – you send them to Egypt.
>
> (Till, 2011)

The former leader of Al Qaeda, Ayman al-Zawahiri, the founder of Al Qaeda in Iraq, Abu Musab al-Zarqawi, the Yemeni-American radical cleric Anwar al-Awlaki, and the former leader of the Islamic State in Iraq and Syria, Abu Bakr al-Baghdadi, were all byproducts of Arab correctional systems that fueled their antagonism toward the region's regimes, hatred for their allies, and commitment to terrorism. Regardless of the regional trends of terrorism and the formerly mentioned protests, there remains an alarming paucity of knowledge on criminology in the Arab world.

Criminology's Rapid Progression

For readers unfamiliar with the discipline, the inattention to criminology in the Arab world might seem a little perplexing. In the first two decades of the 21st century, the field of criminology progressed and branched into numerous subfields. Citizens have grown to be critical of the current approaches to criminal justice, and protests against injustices have erupted worldwide. The onset of COVID-19 has severely impacted the world economy (Nicola et al., 2020) and has amplified many structural disparities in criminal justice. The death of George Floyd at the hands of a white police officer in the United States was the catalyst for global protests against racial discrimination, systematic inequalities, and police brutality. The nation-wide American protests from the Black Lives Matter movement spread to the favelas of Rio de Janeiro over the police killing of 14-year-old João Pedro Matos Pinto to the banlieues of Paris, where police officers assaulted and racially abused Michel Zecler and inspired the revitalization of the campaign in Lagos to

4 *Why Arab Criminology?*

end the Special Anti-Robbery Squad (SARS) over its track record for abuse, torture, and extra-judicial executions. Far earlier than the Arab Spring and contemporary international protests, academics long excoriated the dominant perspectives that recur as the preeminent approaches or solutions to contemporary criminal justice problems. Criminology has largely marginalized non-Western viewpoints, with scholars from the United States and the United Kingdom leading in the production of knowledge with the most citations in the field (Wright, 2002; Aas, 2012; Bosworth & Hoyle, 2012; Lee & Laidler, 2013; Cohn et al., 2017). The discipline has constructed a hegemonic uniformity, with the American system at the pinnacle. This hierarchy has entangled ethnocentrism with criminology by positioning non-Western knowledge as unsophisticatedly or regressively at the bottom and thus belonging in the periphery. Meanwhile, the field situates Western positions as universal and, at times, the only solution to success. Moosavi (2018, p. 231) identifies six factors of why criminology remains a fundamentally Western-centric enterprise as a result of (1) Western scholars' lack of reflexivity in upholding Orientalist views of the Other; (2) non-Western scholars educated in the West that have emulated and reproduced Western-centric criminology without problematizing or challenging the approaches; (3) socio-political factors faced by non-Western scholars that curtail non-Western scholarship; (4) research published in non-English languages that exclude it from the lingua franca of academia; (5) the neoliberalism and corporatization of academia that are not conducive to research exploring non-Western approaches; and finally, (6) inequalities that remain in academia, publishers, organizations, and universities that have excluded non-Western scholars. According to Moosavi (2018), Western domination will persist until scholars recognize and challenge these issues. The field has essentially excluded Arab criminology's experiences and perspectives, and this book will demonstrate how Arab criminology can contribute to, permeate, and transform mainstream Western-centric criminology.

Framing Arab Criminology

In recent years, criminology has expanded beyond the West and unto multiple regions worldwide. Europe, North America, and Australasia prevail over criminology with long-established organizations, university programs, books, and journals. The 20th century, in particular, has been dominated by Chicago, the University of Pennsylvania, and Columbia as well as other institutions in the United States (Cullen et al., 2011). Latin America's colonial ties to Europe and the United States blended the latest ideas from both continents. Since the First Latin American Congress of Criminology in

Why Arab Criminology? 5

1938, numerous societies, institutions, policies, books, and journals have flourished in Latin America (Del Olmo, 1999; Salvatore & Aguirre, 2010). Today, criminology has proliferated in many parts of the world. The Caribbean nations established the *Caribbean Journal of Criminology & Social Psychology* with calls for establishing Caribbean criminology in the 1990s (Bennett & Lynch, 1996; Cain, 1996). African criminology is also well documented (Clifford, 1974; Brillon, 1985; Cohen, 1986; Igbinovia, 1989) with the *African Journal of Criminology and Justice Studies*, *Acta Criminologica: African Journal of Criminology & Victimology*, *African Journal of Law and Criminology*, and the *Africa Journal of Crime and Justice*, journals focused predominantly on criminology in sub-Saharan countries. Likewise, Chinese, Korean, Japanese, and Indian criminologies have long-established histories in Asia. The continent has many criminological organizations like the Asian Criminological Society that hold annual conferences, publications, and numerous journals, including the *Asian Journal of Criminology* (Liu, 2009; Belknap, 2016).

Both African and Asian criminologies have largely overlooked criminological knowledge from Arab nations in the transcontinental MENA (the Middle East and North Africa) region. The deep-rooted cultural, historical, legal, linguistic, and political connections bind the nations in the Arab world far more than the "convenient geopolitical constructs" (Liu, 2009, p. 75) that define African, Asian, Caribbean, Latin American, North American, and European criminologies. This book will explicate arguments for creating a distinct Arab criminology subfield. Unlike scholars in political science, economics, anthropology, and sociology, criminologists continue to shockingly neglect the study of crime and criminal justice in the Arab world despite the region's strategic significance in international geopolitical issues, from the protests of the Arab Spring, War on Terror, revolutions, and conflicts to the ongoing refugee crisis.

In establishing this subfield, Arab criminology will aspire to southernize (Hogg et al., 2017; Carrington et al., 2019) and decolonize (Agozino, 2004; Blagg & Anthony, 2019). Southern criminology is a theoretical framework designed to recognize the hierarchical production of knowledge that heavily advances theories, concepts, and methods specific to the Global North (Connell, 2007). The approach recognizes the North's predominance in academia, conferences, publishers, journals, and scientific knowledge (Graham et al., 2011; Hogg et al., 2017). According to the authors Carrington et al. (2016), Southern criminology is a perspective that would decolonize, democratize, and globalize the discipline through the promotion, inclusion, and expansion of Southern issues shaped by a variety of non-Western historical, social, cultural, political, and religious factors as sources of criminological knowledge. The criminological issues that endure in Africa,

6 *Why Arab Criminology?*

Asia, Latin America, and Oceania differ in the levels of corruption, violence, poverty, and political instability that all factor into the study of crime. The dominance of the Global North on research has created a hegemony of knowledge based on the experiences of very few specific regions of the world (Connell, 2007; Faraldo-Cabana, 2018). The southernization of criminology is an agenda that claims to resist Northern hegemony and biases and expose its limits through Southern perspectives that foster new global projects and narrow the current gaps (Carrington et al., 2016, 2019).

Advocates perceive Southern criminology as an opportunity for both the North and South to communicate and exchange knowledge rather than dismiss, criticize, or discredit Northern contributions to criminology. Critics of Southern criminology, however, worry that the subfield might remain uncritical of Northern criminology (Brown, 2017), fail to uphold Southern or Indigenous viewpoints (Cunneen, 2018), or unsuccessfully decolonize criminology (Moosavi, 2019). Travers (2017) even argues that Southern criminology is an impossible enterprise due to the dissimilarities and grand diversity between regions, cultures, religions, and languages in the Global South. He additionally asks whether the Global South should be generalized to advance a political view and whether it will ever be possible to imagine alternative global criminologies. However, for many, Southern criminology's mission of inclusivity and the democratization of knowledge might not generate anything new or amend the current disparities (Carrington et al., 2019).

Other academics also acknowledge the Global North's authority over the discipline and embrace an unreservedly post-colonial approach that acknowledges colonialism's legacy and actively seeks to decolonize criminology (Agozino, 2004, Chakrabarty, 2007; Connell, 2007; Mignolo, 2012; de Sousa Santos, 2015). These scholars acknowledge colonization as a history of oppression, slavery, violence, and dehumanization that benefited the Global North to the South's detriment. Contrasting Southern criminology, these scholars argue that the field's attempts to southernize will fail due to the North's hegemony over academia that stems from the vast colonization process that spanned centuries. Proponents argue that a long-term agenda is needed to decolonize and shift social sciences to more wide-ranging geographies. Southern criminology's call to build bridges, they contend, does not directly confront the historical origins of social science as a tool for colonialism and imperialism in the Global South that prolongs perceptions of a dysfunctional South in need of Northern proficiency. Epistemicide, or the destruction and appropriation of knowledge of the colonized, has invariably affected the global South as described by Kenyan academic Wa Thiong'o (2009, p. 21): "Get a few natives, empty their hard disk of a previous memory, and download into them a software of European memory."

The decolonization of criminology calls for the reassertion of "epistemologies of the South" (de Sousa Santos, 2015) to counter the Northern hegemony over the social sciences' epistemology.

Blagg and Anthony (2019) are skeptics arguing that Southern criminology perpetuates the status quo. The authors insist that the southernization approach will not generate new perspectives but rather preserve Northern supremacy. They regard Southern criminology as nothing more than a defensive response, an exoneration of Northern hegemony that is now being attacked and threatened by post-colonial and decolonization approaches in the South in what Agozino (2010, pp. ii, vii, xv) describes as criminology's "control freak" inclinations. The authors (2019) claim that the intent to decolonize criminology is not about reconciliation or highlighting deficiencies in the South. They reject the view that colonization is just another variable in the study of criminology and refuse to accept the position that colonization was merely a historical event that took place long ago with no direct contemporary implications. Instead, decolonizing criminology should challenge and delegitimize Northern hegemony. Other disciplines have long recognized the colonial roots of contemporary knowledge, and even in criminology, post-colonial critiques are somewhat addressed (Agozino, 2004, 2010; Cunneen, 2011). Therefore, Blagg and Anthony (2019) propose that criminology expands to other worldviews with strategies of Indigenous refusal, resistance, and resurgence in a discipline built on Western imperialism and colonialism. They contend that greater inclusion of non-Western scholarship within criminological discussions is central to the pursuit of decolonizing criminology, and a failure to address these issues "will eventually create a crisis of legitimacy at the level of theory and practice" (2019, p. 16).

The contributions of Southern and decolonized criminology will inspire and shape Arab criminology. Though there are differences in the two paradigms, both recognize that 'normal science' preserves and reinforces Northern approaches, theories, research, and perspectives. Arab criminology should adopt the points recommended by Southern advocates in utilizing Northern and Southern collaborative research. Comparable to Liu's (2017) agenda for Asian criminology, the region must adapt and test Northern methodological/theoretical orientations to "evaluate their feasibility; and generalizing them to a broader scope" (2017, p. 77) with the same academic standards of other criminologies that must be "creating and incorporating new concepts that are faithful to the social realities" (2017, p. 77) of Arab societies. The subfield will also incorporate interdisciplinary, multidisciplinary, and transdisciplinary approaches that embrace knowledge from anthropology, sociology, history, political science, and other social sciences to advance further and build peer-reviewed research, policies, and programs. Although Arab criminology has been largely ignored and forced to the periphery, the subfield should recognize, affirm, and deconstruct contemporary criminological methods and strategically establish the subfield without altogether rejecting everything Northern. The Southern criminological agenda that communicates and exchanges knowledge with the Global North will help the subfield develop concepts, theories, and methodologies grounded in the Arab world (Liu, 2017) that challenge and evolve conventional criminological perspectives.

Contrary to Southern criminology, this subfield and the literature on decolonized criminology consider the discipline's fragmentation as one manner to foster knowledge democratization. The Arab world is distinct in its cultures, religions, history, and languages compared to other Global South regions (Travers, 2017), yet there has been little to no interest in making Northern criminology applicable to Arab nations. The decolonization of criminology is central to countering ethnocentrism and the perceived universality of Northern perspectives. The decolonization of criminology is a consequential endeavor for Arab criminology due to deep-rooted Northern misconceptions and Orientalist perceptions.

Orientalism (Said, 1978, p. 2) is the portrayal of Arabs and Arab cultures in an exaggerated and distorted manner when compared to those in the West or "a style of thought based upon an ontological and epistemological distinction made between 'the Orient' and (most of the time) 'the Occident.'" Edward Said, one of the founders of post-colonial studies and author of the renowned text *Orientalism*, further states that Orientalism is "the basic distinction between East and West as the starting point for elaborate theories, epics, novels, social descriptions, and political accounts concerning the Orient, its people, customs, 'mind,' destiny and so on" (1978, pp. 2–3). This exaggeration of difference has been an unfortunate part of Northern perspectives of crime, violence, and justice, with misperceptions of Arabs as naturally violent, irrational, primitive, childlike, monolithic, exotic, sensuous, and inferior (Said, 1978). Orientalism is one of the main challenges facing the literature on criminology in the Arab world, with insights into and depictions of "severed hands, religious police, and *qadi* justice" (Crystal, 2001, p. 469). These misrepresentations pervert knowledge of the region and produce an inaccurate criminological analysis.

According to Said (1978), Orientalist ideology morally justified European imperialism, colonialism, interventionism, and subjugation through the process of 'othering' and dehumanizing Arabs. Said explained: "Colonial rule was justified in advance by Orientalism, rather than after the fact" (1978, p. 39). Orientalism was instrumental for rationalizing exploitive policies that had long-standing consequences on the colonized (Blunt & McEwan, 2003). The perceptions of the inferiority of the Arab world vindicated epistemicidical policies that stripped the region of knowledge from its history, culture, and languages replacing them with European ones. The 'White Man's Burden,' '*Mission Civilisatrice*,' and other claims of civilizing and modernizing Indigenous people concealed colonialism's exploitative nature through strategies that still serve Western countries' interests today. For example, the U.S. War on Terror in Afghanistan and Iraq were "justified through terms such as democratization, restructuring and development" (Malik, 2006, p. 39). Orientalist discourses on altruistic liberation of women in veils, burqas, and niqabs masked the Bush administration's obsession with oil, war profiteering by numerous companies from the military–industrial complex, and the neoconservative desire of establishing American ascendancy.

Orientalism, terrorism, and the wars of the past two decades have spurred the multi-billion-dollar Islamophobia industry (Lean & Esposito, 2012) or what has been labeled as the "green scare" (Kumar, 2012). Pseudo-experts and analysts with absolutely no background or academic training, immersion in the region, or any study or fluency in the Arabic language are some of the most common disseminators of Islamophobia that neither advance knowledge nor promote any form of understanding of the region (Salaita, 2006; Ali et al., 2011; Ekman, 2015). Many of the publications on the region circulating in mainstream bookstores reinforce preconceived Orientalist notions that regenerate clichés of Arab crime, violence, and corruption. The Islamic religion, or what Islamophobes termed as 'Islamofascism,' is perceived as a nefarious political ideology comparable to Fascism, Nazism, or Communism (Hibbard, 2010). These approaches position Arab and Islamic culture in problematic, violent, or terroristic categories and are understood only through the security prism with full endorsement by Orientalist academics, institutions, think tanks, and government officials.

One of the most prominent examples of this form of Orientalism in academia emanated from Bernard Lewis, the late Professor Emeritus of Near Eastern Studies at Princeton University. Known as "the West's leading interpreter of the Middle East" (Abrahmson, 2007), Lewis's work demonstrates the worse examples of Orientalism that has prevailed in Northern perspectives of the Arab world. As a renowned scholar of the region, Lewis claimed that "generalizing about Islamic civilization may be difficult and at times in a sense dangerous, it is not impossible and may in some ways be useful" (Lewis, 2004, pp. 3–4). These scholars' generalizations of the Arab world have not remained only in academic circles but have significantly influenced foreign policies in the MENA region. During the Bush administration's invasion of Iraq, Lewis became the ideologue that intellectually legitimized the war by declaring that "[e]ither we bring them freedom, or they destroy us" and that Arabs only understand the language of fear and violence (Thomas, 2003), as well as describing the Iraqi people as becoming celebratory and rejoiceful once the United States invaded (Martin, 2018).

Another disturbing example is Raphael Patai's (2004) *The Arab Mind*, which seeks to define the mindsets and culture of millions of citizens in the Arab world. Although the book stereotypically characterizes the 'mind' of all Arabs across time and space, Patai's (2004) work became the Bible of Arab behavior for American politicians and was the source for the sexual abuse and torture suffered by prisoners in the Iraqi Abu Ghraib scandal. As Hersh (2004) explains, "The notion that Arabs are particularly vulnerable to sexual humiliation became a talking point among pro-war Washington conservatives in the months before the March 2003 invasion of Iraq.... One book that was frequently cited was *The Arab Mind*."

There are limitations in Said's Orientalism; critics claim that he made the same generalizations about the Occident as he accused the Orientalists. Ahmad (1992) wrote a lengthy critique of Said's representation of a unified European perspective that has maintained the same perceptions of the Orient for centuries. Even Lewis (1982) responded to Said's treatment of Orientalists as a unified whole by pointing to the contributions of German, Dutch, and other European Orientalists that contributed to knowledge on the Arab world and advocated for Arab causes but whose scholarly work had no benefit for colonial powers. Nevertheless, Said's work has been prolific in post-colonial studies and is a critique that can be combined with the balanced approach of Southern criminology to decolonize criminology in the Arab world. The Western universalism that Said exposed is still regrettably prevalent in criminology. Since Said, there have been various branches of Orientalism (Pavan Kumar, 2012), including military (Porter, 2009), American (Obeidat, 1998), internal (Mazumdar et al., 2010), parallel (Koshy, 2008), pulp (Irwin, 2006), techno (Niu, 2008), counter (Scanlan, 2001), and economic (Latham, 1999) that can contribute to the sub-discipline of Arab criminology.

The chapters of this book aim to frame an agenda for the subfield of Arab criminology through critical scholarship that would subvert Northern preconceptions, myths, and fears of the MENA region. The agenda will establish new epistemes and narratives that counter the region's Northern hegemonic perceptions with empirical research and sociological reflexivity that confronts the Orientalist stereotypes of the Arab world (Said, 1978; Kumar, 2010; Ventura, 2017). Through the contributions previously mentioned, Arab criminology will challenge the assumptions that portray the Arab world as powerlessly crying out for help and liberation from the Western world and, at the same time, will approach criminology in a critical unapologetic manner.

The Parameters of Arab Identity

There are debates among scholars in ethnic studies in conceptualizing Arab ethnicity and racial identity (Ajrouch & Jamal, 2007; Jamal et al., 2008; Webb, 2016). With over 400 million citizens, the Arab world stretches across North Africa and West Asia. The region is not monolithic and consists of diverse races, ethnicities, languages, religions, and cultures. Arab nations comprise systems ranging from absolute and constitutional monarchies, sultanates, emirates, and republics. The diversity of the Arab world is a challenge when applying criminological ideas that originate in other regions of the world. Many unfamiliar with the Arab world's diversity ponder the factors that connect such diverse people in formulating a mutual cultural identity and collective memory.

The conceptualization of Arab criminology originates in the political ideology that developed around pan-Arabism or the belief that all Arabs belong to and should strive for a unified demarcated territory as one nation (Dawisha, 2003). However, pan-Arabism originated in the 19th-century *annahda* movement, the ideology formalized in the early 20th century during Ottoman domination, European colonization, the migration of Jewish settlers to Palestine, and the founding of the Arab Ba'ath Party, a political fusion of Arab nationalism and pan-Arabism (Walters, 2017). Pan-Arabism, at the time, was heavily influenced by the international growth of national movements worldwide, especially in Europe after the world wars. The ideology called for an imagined transnational community transcending tribal, religious, or national affiliations and positioning Arabness as the primary identity. This secularized identity assimilated Muslims, Christians, Jews, atheists, and other religious groups under the umbrella of Arab identity that distinguished Arabs from Turkish and European colonizers (Choueiri, 2000). The ideology was further propagated when Arab nations were granted independence and new political parties competed for power in the newly formed sovereign states.

During this period, Arab nationalists with the slogan *umma 'arabiyya waahida dhat risala khaalida* (one Arab nation with an eternal message) discussed and debated which political ideologies would guide pan-Arabism into the creation of a strong, independent, and unified Arab nation (Salem, 1994). It was only natural that the popular Egyptian president Jamal Abdel Nasser would become the undeniable leader of the pan-Arab movement and potential political consolidator of the Arab world. Nasser's opposition to European imperialism; perceived victory over Israel, the United Kingdom, and France in the Suez Crisis; and support for liberation movements in the Arab world, Africa, Asia, and Latin America made him one of the most popular Arab figures internationally. Nasser formed the United Arab Republic through a political union between Egypt, Syria, and Yemen that only lasted a couple of years. Influenced by Nasser, the Libyan leader Qaddafi attempted to merge Libya, Egypt, Sudan, and Syria into a unified Federation of Arab Republics that lasted for about five years. In the years since, Arab leaders continue to perform homage to pan-Arabism while scheming for power without any genuine concern for Arab unification. In due course, Arab nations abandoned any discussions on unity and focused solely on cooperating regionally and across the Arab world (Dawisha, 2003).

Pan-Arabism has had a lasting effect on a region that continues to share a similar "language, ethnicity, history, customs, and political aspirations" (Choueiri, 2000, p. 91). Although Ba'athist ideology is politically obsolete after Saddam Hussein's death and the near-destruction of Bashar Assad's Syria, the impact of pan-Arabism still resonates in the Arab world. The Arab League, one of the last remnants of Arab nationalism, establishes the parameters of Arab ethnic and racial identity. The Arab League was formed in 1945 with six Arab countries to align, collaborate, safeguard their sovereignty, and pursue member states' interests (Pact of the League of Arab States, 1945). The Arab League currently has 22 countries and 5 observer states. According to the Arab League, national self-identification with the Arabic language and culture defines a citizen's/country's membership. These parameters in conceptualizing Arab identity are what academics, politicians, and policymakers have used in politics and academia (Mohamedou, 2016; Worrall, 2017; Sepielak et al., 2019).

Outline of the Chapters

As explained, Arab nations have commonalities that do not exist in other forms of regional criminologies. The shared languages, legal systems, cultures, and history will help conceptualize the subfield of Arab criminology. The rest of the chapters will lay out the case for Arab criminology by examining several components. This chapter briefly addressed, *Why Arab Criminology?* The chapter presented factors that contributed to the failure of including the Arab world in much of criminological research. The chapter then briefly discussed the theoretical contributions of Southern and decolonization criminologies and their potential impact on Arab criminology, focusing on how the decolonization research can confront Orientalist and Islamophobic tropes of the region. The chapter concluded with a broad definition of Arab identity through the parameters established by the Arab League.

The second chapter will examine Islamic law and the Arab World. This chapter will argue that one focal feature of Arab societies that distinguishes

Arab criminology from others is the prominent role of Islamic law in shaping the legal and political confines of what constitutes crime, justice, and punishment. Mainstream criminological approaches have little to no background or understanding of Islamic jurisprudence. Along with explaining the complexities of Islamic law and the diverse legal traditions in the Arab world, the chapter will contend that an Arab criminology subfield would better appreciate Islam's intricate impact on law, crime, and criminal justice. The chapter will further discuss the relationship between Islamic law and the administration of justice so that the reader can better understand the significant role of religion in the study of Arab criminology.

The third chapter details and substantiates the claim that Arab nations' historical, political, and cultural commonalities provide the sub-discipline with the foundation for critically understanding crime and criminal justice in the region. We situate the development of the region's criminal justice systems in historical pre-colonial, colonial, and post-colonial political and cultural frameworks. The chapter will reveal the enduring impact Arab collective history has on contemporary political and cultural institutions while manifesting how these interrelated commonalities of the Arab world can provide the field of criminology with new paradigmatic views of these spaces.

The fourth chapter will address the importance of race and gender as sociodemographic variables in the development of Arab criminology. It will build on the existing contributions from Northern and Southern criminology to discuss how race, gender, and crime from within the Arab world can contribute to the ongoing development and growth of Arab criminology. In doing so, the chapter will discuss the minimal research that has been produced in these topics and then discuss the importance of localizing the study of race, gender, and crime from within the Arab world to produce new theoretical and applied possibilities.

The fifth chapter examines transnational crimes in the Arab world, highlighting the specters of terrorism, drug trafficking, and human smuggling/trafficking as areas of high priority for research. After assessing these transnational crimes, each section analyzes the strategies displayed by Arab governments, presenting valuable lessons and policies for the international community. Furthermore, the chapter explores the collaborative efforts between Arab nations and international organizations in addressing transnational crime with an emphasis on the conventions passed by the Arab League and the United Nations Office on Drugs and Crime's Regional Program for the Arab states to strengthen criminal justice systems. Finally, the chapter identifies the potential research prospects for the subdiscipline of Arab criminology.

The last chapter, 'Moving Forward,' outlines the future of Arab criminology. The chapter identifies the requirements for establishing Arab criminology and details the manner in which local, regional, and international researchers can collaborate, develop, and expand the subfield. The authors detail the numerous challenges and opportunities in Arab criminology. To move forward Arab criminology requires an empirical-based research agenda that builds on the conceptual frameworks of mainstream criminologies that will conceive new orientations for the Arab world. Finally, the chapter urges academics in the subdiscipline to organize future conferences and peer-reviewed journals on criminology in the Arab world that would provide a medium for the exchange of information and advance/expand the study of criminology, criminal justice, and the region's legal system.

References

Aas, K. F. (2012). The earth is one but the world is not: Criminological theory and its geopolitical divisions. *Theoretical Criminology*, *16*(1), 5–20.

Abrahmson, J. L. (2007, June 8). Will the west – and the United States – go the distance? *American Diplomacy*. https://americandiplomacy.web.unc.edu/2007/06/will-the-west-and-the-united-states-go-the-distance/

Agozino, B. (2004). Imperialism, crime and criminology: Towards the decolonisation of criminology. *Crime, Law and Social Change*, *41*(4), 343–358.

Agozino, B. (2010). What is criminology? A control-freak discipline! *African Journal of Criminology and Justice Studies*, *4*, 1–20.

Ahmad, A. (1992). *In theory: Classes, nations, literatures*. Verso.

Ajrouch, K. J., & Jamal, A. (2007). Assimilating to a white identity: The case of Arab Americans. *International Migration Review*, *41*, 860–879.

Ali, W., Clifton, E., Duss, M., Fang, L., Keyes, S., & Shakir, F. (2011). *Fear, Inc: The roots of the Islamophobia network in America*. Center for American Progress.

Bayat, A. (2013). The Arab spring and its surprises. *Development and Change*, *44*(3), 587–601.

Belknap, J. (2016). Asian criminology's expansion and advancement of research and crime control practices. *Asian Journal of Criminology*, *11*(4), 249–264.

Bennett, R., & Lynch, J. P. (1996). Towards a Caribbean criminology: Prospects and problems. *Caribbean Journal of Criminology and Social Psychology*, *1*(1), 8–37.

Bjørgo, T. (Ed.). (2004). *Root causes of terrorism: Myths, reality and ways forward*. Routledge.

Bjørgo, T., & Silke, A. (2018). Root causes of terrorism. In A. Silke (Ed.), *Routledge handbook of terrorism and counterterrorism* (pp. 57–65). Routledge.

Blagg, H., & Anthony, T. (2019). *Decolonising criminology: Imagining justice in a post-colonial world*. Springer Nature.

Blunt, A., & McEwan, C. (Eds.). (2003). *Post-colonial geographies*. Bloomsbury Publishing.

Bosworth, M., & Hoyle, C. (Eds.). (2012). *What is criminology?* Oxford University Press.

Brillon, Y. (1985). *Crime, justice and culture in Black Africa: An ethno-criminological study. Cashier no. 3*. Centre International de Criminologie Comparee, Universite de Montreal.
Brown, D. W. (2017). *A new introduction to Islam*. John Wiley & Sons.
Cain, M. (1996). Crime and criminology in the Caribbean introduction. *Caribbean Quarterly, 42*(2–3), v–xx.
Carrington, K., Dixon, B., Fonseca, D., Goyes, D. R., Liu, J., & Zysman, D. (2019). Criminologies of the global south: Critical reflections. *Critical Criminology, 27*(1), 163–189.
Carrington, K., Hogg, R., Scott, J., Sozzo, M., & Walters, R. (2019). *Southern criminology*. Routledge.
Carrington, K., Sozzo, M., & Hogg, R. (2016). Southern criminology. *British Journal of Criminology, 56*, 257.
Chakrabarty, D. (2007). *Provincializing Europe: Post-colonial thought and difference* (2nd ed.). Princeton University Press.
Choueiri, Y. (2000). *Arab nationalism: A history: Nation and state in the Arab world*. Blackwell Publishers.
Clifford, W. (1974). *An introduction to African criminology*. Oxford University Press.
Cohen, S. (1986). Bandits, rebels or criminals: African history and western criminology' in Africa. *Journal of the International African Institute, 56*(4), 468–483.
Cohn, E. G., Farrington, D. P., & Iratzoqui, A. (2017). Changes in the most-cited scholars and works over 25 years: The evolution of the field of criminology and criminal justice. *Journal of Criminal Justice Education, 28*(1), 25–51.
Connell, R. (2007). *Southern theory: Social science and the global dynamics of knowledge*. Polity.
Crawford, N. C. (2019, November 13). United States budgetary costs and obligations of post-9/11 wars through FY2020: $6.4 trillion. *Watson Institute Brown University*. https://watson.brown.edu/costsofwar/figures/2019/budgetary-costs-post-911-wars-through-fy2020-64-trillion
Crenshaw, M. (1981). The causes of terrorism. *Comparative Politics, 13*(4), 379–399.
Crystal, J. (2001). Criminal justice in the Middle East. *Journal of Criminal Justice, 29*, 469–482.
Cullen, F. T., Myer, A. J., Adler, F., & Jonson, C. L. (Eds.). (2011). *The origins of American criminology: Advances in criminological theory* (Vol. 1). Transaction Publishers.
Cunneen, C. (2011). Post-colonial perspectives for criminology. In M. Bosworth & C. Hoyle (Eds.), *What is criminology?* Oxford University Press.
Cunneen, C. (2018). Indigenous challenges for southern criminology. In K. Carrington, R. Hogg, J. Scott, & M. Sozzo (Eds.), *The Palgrave handbook of criminology and the global south* (pp. 19–40). Palgrave Macmillan.
Dawisha, A. (2003). *Rise and fall of Arab nationalism*. Princeton University Press.
Del Olmo, R. (1999). The development of criminology in Latin America. *Social Justice, 26*(2), 19–45.

de Sousa Santos, B. (2015). *Epistemologies of the south: Justice against epistemicide*. Routledge.
Ekman, M. (2015). Online Islamophobia and the politics of fear: Manufacturing the green scare. *Ethnic and Racial Studies, 38*, 1986–2002.
Faraldo-Cabana, P. (2018). Research excellence and anglophone dominance: The case of law, criminology and social science. In K. Carrington, R. Hogg, J. Scott, & M. Sozzo (Eds.), *The Palgrave handbook of criminology and the global south* (pp. 163–181). Palgrave Macmillan.
Gause, F. G. (2011). Why Middle East studies missed the Arab spring: The myth of authoritarian stability. *Foreign Affairs*, 81–90.
Graham, M., Hale, S. A., & Stephens, M. (2011). *Geographies of the world's knowledge*. Convoco! Edition.
Hersh, S. M. (2004, May 16). The gray zone: How a secret pentagon program came to Abu Ghraib. *The New Yorker*. www.newyorker.com/archive/2004/05/24/040524fa_fact
Hibbard, S. (2010). "Islamo-fascism" as an ideological discourse. *Journal of Islamic Law and Culture, 12*(1), 10–23.
Hogg, R., Scott, J., & Sozzo, M. (2017). 'Editor's introduction', special edition: Southern criminology – guest editors' introduction. *International Journal for Crime, Justice and Social Democracy, 6*(1), 1–7.
Human Rights Watch. (2010, June 24). Egypt: Prosecute police in beating death. *Human Rights Watch*. www.hrw.org/news/2010/06/24/egypt-prosecute-police-beating-death
Human Rights Watch. (2011, June 1). "We've never seen such horror": Crimes against humanity by Syrian security forces. *Human Rights Watch*. www.hrw.org/report/2011/06/01/weve-never-seen-such-horror/crimes-against-humanity-syrian-security-forces
Igbinovia, P. E. (1989). Criminology in Africa. *International Journal of Offender Therapy and Comparative Criminology, 33*(2), v–x.
Irfan, A., Sulaiman, Z., & Liaquat, H. (2020). Root causes of terrorism: A systematic review of past decade. *Journal of Public Value and Administrative Insight, 3*(4), 183–199. https://doi.org/10.31580/jpvai.v3i4.1803
Irwin, R. (2006). *For lust of knowing: The orientalists and their enemies*. Penguin.
Jamal, A. A., Naber, N., & Naber, N. C. (Eds.). (2008). *Race and Arab Americans before and after 9/11: From invisible citizens to visible subjects*. Syracuse University Press.
Koshy, S. (2008). Post-colonial studies after 9/11: A response to Ali Behdad. *American Literary History, 20*(1–2), 300–303.
Krieger, T., & Meierrieks, D. (2011). What causes terrorism? *Public Choice, 147*(1), 3–27.
Kumar, D. (2010). Framing Islam: The resurgence of orientalism during the bush II era. *Journal of Communication Inquiry, 34*, 254–277.
Kumar, D. (2012). *Islamophobia and the politics of empire*. Haymarket Books.
LaFree, G., & Dugan, L. (2015). How has criminology contributed to the study of terrorism since 9/11? In *Terrorism and counterterrorism today* (Vol. 20, pp. 1–23). Emerald Group.

LaFree, G., & Freilich, J. (2016). Bringing criminology into the study of terrorism. In G. LaFree & J. Freilich (Eds.), *The handbook of the criminology of terrorism* (pp. 3–14). Wiley. https://doi.org/10.1002/9781118923986

Latham, A. (1999). Response to Woo-Cumings. *Macalester International*, 7(1), 19.

Lean, N., & Esposito, J. L. (2012). *The Islamophobia industry: How the right manufactures fear of Muslims*. Pluto Press.

Lee, M., & Laidler, K. J. (2013). Doing criminology from the periphery: Crime and punishment in Asia. *Theoretical Criminology*, 17, 141–157.

Lewis, B. (1982). The question of "orientalism." *The New York Review*, 49–56.

Lewis, B. (2004). *The crisis of Islam: Holy war and unholy terror*. Random House Incorporated.

Liu, J. (2009). Asian criminology – challenges, opportunities, and directions. *Asian Journal of Criminology*, 4(1), 1–9.

Liu, J. (2017). The new Asian paradigm: A relational approach. In J. Liu, M. Travers, & L. Y. C. Chang (Eds.), *Comparative criminology in Asia* (pp. 17–32). Springer.

Malik, I. H. (2006). *Crescent between cross and star; Muslims and the west after 9/11*. Oxford University Press.

Martin, D. (2018, May 21). Bernard Lewis, influential scholar of Islam, is dead at 101. *New York Times*. www.nytimes.com/2018/05/21/obituaries/bernard-lewis-islam-scholar-dies.html

Mazumdar, S., Kaiwar, V., & Labica, T. (Eds.). (2010). *From orientalism to postcolonialism: Asia, Europe and the lineages of difference* (Vol. 20). Routledge.

Mignolo, W. (2012). *Local histories/global designs: Coloniality, subaltern knowledges, and border thinking*. Princeton University Press.

Mohamedou, M. M. O. (2016). Arab agency and the U.N. project: The league of Arab states between universality and regionalism. *Third World Quarterly*, 37, 1219–1233.

Moosavi, L. (2018). Decolonising criminology: Syed Hussein Alatas on crimes of the powerful. *Critical Criminology*, 1–14.

Moosavi, L. (2019). A friendly critique of 'Asian criminology' and 'southern criminology'. *The British Journal of Criminology*, 59(2), 257–275.

Nicola, M., Alsafi, Z., Sohrabi, C., Kerwan, A., Al-Jabir, A., Iosifidis, C., Agha, M., & Agha, R. (2020). The socio-economic implications of the coronavirus and COVID-19 pandemic: A review. *International Journal of Surgery*, 78, 185–193. https://doi.org/10.1016/j.ijsu.2020.04.018

Niu, G. A. (2008). Techno-orientalism, nanotechnology, posthumans, and post-posthumans in Neal Stephenson's and Linda Nagata's science fiction. *Melus*, 33(4), 73–96.

Obeidat, M. (1998). *American literature and orientalism*. Klaus Schwarz.

Ouassini, N., & Ouassini, A. (2020). Criminology in the Arab world: Misconceptions, nuances and future prospects. *The British Journal of Criminology*, 60(3), 519–536.

Pact of the League of Arab States. (1945, March 22). Yale Lillian Goldman law library. *The Avalon Project*. https://avalon.law.yale.edu/20th_century/arableag.asp

Patai, R. (2004). *The Arab mind*. Hatherleigh Press.
Pavan Kumar, M. (2012). Introduction: Orientalism (s) after 9/11. *Journal of Postcolonial Writing*, *48*(3), 233–240.
Porter, P. (2009). *Military orientalism: Eastern war through western eyes*. Columbia University Press.
Said, E. (1978). *Orientalism*. Vintage Books.
Salaita, S. (2006). *Anti-Arab racism in the USA: Where it comes from and what it means for politics today*. Pluto Press.
Salem, P. (1994). *Bitter legacy: Ideology and politics in the Arab world*. Syracuse University Press.
Salvatore, R. D., & Aguirre, C. (Eds.). (2010). *The birth of the penitentiary in Latin America: Essays on criminology, prison reform, and social control, 1830–1940*. University of Texas Press.
Scanlan, M. (2001). *Plotting terror: Novelists and terrorists in contemporary fiction*. University of Virginia Press.
Sepielak, K., Wladyka, D., & Yaworsky, W. (2019). Unsung interpreters: The jumbled practice of language translation in contemporary field research – A study of anthropological field sites in the Arab league countries. *Language and Intercultural Communication*, *19*, 1–17.
Stack, L. (2011, May 31). Video of tortured boy's corpse deepens anger in Syria. *New York Times*. www.nytimes.com/2011/05/31/world/middleeast/31syria.html
Thomas, E. (2003, March 30). The 12 year itch. *Newsweek*. www.newsweek.com/12-year-itch-132309
Till, B. (2011, February 1). A note on Egyptian torture. *The Atlantic*. www.theatlantic.com/international/archive/2011/02/a-note-on-egyptian-torture/70476/
Travers, M. (2017). The idea of a southern criminology. *International Journal of Comparative and Applied Criminal Justice*, *43*, 1–12.
Ventura, L. (2017). The "Arab spring" and orientalist stereotypes: The role of orientalism in the narration of the revolts in the Arab world. *Interventions*, *19*, 282–297.
Walters, K. (2017). Arab Nationalism and/as Language Ideology. In E. Benmamoun & R. Bassiouney (Eds.), *The Routledge Handbook of Arabic Linguistics* (pp. 475–487). Routledge, Taylor & Francis Group.
Wa Thiong'o, N. (2009). *Something torn and new: An African renaissance*. Basic Civitas Books.
Webb, P. (2016). *Imagining the Arabs: Arab identity and the rise of Islam*. Edinburgh University Press.
Worrall, J. (2017). *International institutions of the Middle East: The GCC, Arab league, and Arab Maghreb Union*. Routledge.
Wright, R. A. (2002). Recent changes in the most-cited scholars in criminal justice textbooks. *Journal of Criminal Justice*, *30*(3), 183–195.

2 The Islamic Legal Tradition

Introduction

The study of Arab criminology requires a rudimentary understanding of Islamic law and an awareness of its place in shaping the current legal and criminal justice systems in the Arab world (Ouassini & Ouassini, 2020). Northern and comparative criminologists rarely study the Islamic legal tradition beyond a historical reference or footnote. The deficiency of a subject elemental to the Arab and Muslim world is detrimental to the discipline. Mainstream criminology remains ill-equipped to examine a religious tradition that has influenced legal systems covering nearly 30% of the world's population. Unlike the Global North, religious institutions perdure in regimes across the Arab world with considerable multifaceted roles in governance (Brown, 2017b). Islamic law today is manifested in variegated practices that only a subfield of Arab criminology would be able to recognize, appreciate, and address. This chapter will assess and discuss the complex relationship and impact of Islam on law, crime, and criminal justice so the reader can acknowledge the significant role of religion in the study of Arab criminology.

The urgency to include the study of Islamic law in Arab criminology emerges from enduring Northern mainstream portrayals and misconceptions of the Islamic legal tradition. The Orientalism that generated the conditions for the West to undertake colonial projects in the Global South continues to prevail in academia, politics, media, and popular culture with familiar modern-day justifications to intervene in and dominate the so-called uncivilized countries and primitive religions of the East. Europe indefinitely perceived the Arab world as the antithesis of the West. From the early spread of Islam to the Crusades and Reconquista, centuries of conflict and competition have shaped negative attitudes about Islam and the portrayal of Muslims that were far from reality. As Europe increased in global power, the Arab lands garnered special attention as conquest objectives, from the Portuguese and Spanish capturing towns across the Maghreb in the 15th century to

DOI:10.4324/9781003169789-2

20 *The Islamic Legal Tradition*

Napoleon's conquest of Egypt and the Levant. The Western development of Arab and Islamic studies further conveyed a direct contempt for those in the region's people, culture, and religions that rationalized colonial projects. In this context, preconceived notions in the West regarded capricious floggings, amputations, stoning, beheadings, and excessive abuses against women as distinct features of Islamic law. The images of an archaic, cruel, and backward Islamic criminal justice system legitimized the invasions and nearly two centuries of colonization.

By the 1960s, the Arab world faced numerous problems as independence did not free the region from influences and structures established by the former colonial powers (Greer, 1987). The inheritance of colonial institutions that imposed a top-down rule preserved the strategies developed to protect the colonial state and control the people. The legal and criminal justice systems became so integrated by European ideals that they became indistinguishable from the pre-colonial systems despite the extensive revolts against these colonial institutions and post-colonial governments. Northern criminology has under-researched and disregarded the historical transformation of Arab legal systems during colonialism. The current Northern approaches are not prepared for or equipped to understand the complexity and influence of the Islamic religion and colonialism on law, crime, justice, and punishment in the Arab world (Cross, 2018; Moosavi, 2018).

This chapter will introduce the reader to pre-colonial Islamic law, its decline during colonization, and its contemporary applications. The chapter will first provide the reader with an introduction to the fundamental concepts of Islamic law. The reader will be able to discern between *shari'a* and *fiqh*, identify the sources of Islamic law, recognize the four schools of Islamic thought, and ascertain between the *hadd*, *qisas*, and *ta'zir* categories of Islamic criminal laws and punishment. The next section will discuss the impact of European legal importations during the colonization of the Arab world. The chapter will conclude with a section on Islamic law's current practices and influences on the modern Arab legal systems. The chapter will demonstrate that Islamic law is one of the main components of Arab criminology, and the establishment of the subfield would be better suited to adequately navigate the intersectionality between Islam, post-colonialism, crime, and the justice system.

The Islamic Legal System

Most people know Islamic law as *shari'a*, a word that means "a path to be followed" or "the path leading to a source" (Robinson, 1982; Doi, 1984; Abdal-Haqq, 2002, p. 33) and refers to a vast body of authoritative guidance on all aspects of a Muslim's life. For Muslims, God is the source of knowledge, faith, worship, and rules on behavior and interactions in society. The *shari'a*, therefore, encompasses *i'tiqadat* (beliefs), *'ibadah* (ritual worship), *adab* (behavior and manners), *mu'amalat* (social affairs), and *'uqubat* (punishments). Traditional scholars distinguish between the former three as fixed compared to the open interpretation allowed in *mu'amalat* and some categories of *'uqubat* (Ramadan, 2001). The perennial aspects of *shari'a* are sacred and eternal as Muslims believe that God is the ultimate lawmaker.

Meanwhile, *fiqh* is open to interpretation and changes according to circumstances and time. Baderin (2005) explains that the *shari'a* is the source, and *fiqh* is the methodologies utilized to derive and apply the laws. The objective of *fiqh* is the scholarly attempt to adopt the *shari'a* in all aspects of life. Although the values of *shari'a* are eternal, the *fiqh* is open to further development, revision, and expansion depending on the circumstances. Islamic law will be used synonymously with *fiqh* in the rest of the chapter.

The *shari'a* derives from four sources that include the Quran, the Sunnah, *ijma'* (consensus from scholars), and *qiyas al fuqaha* (analogical deduction by jurists) (Kamali, 2008). Muslims believe the Quran is the final word-for-word revelation from God sent to the Prophet Mohammed. The Quran contains over 6,000 verses, with only a few hundred addressing legal matters. As the primary source for *shari'a*, Muslims completely accept its authenticity and believe the Quran provides the solutions to any questions on faith and conduct. However, the Sunnah of the Prophet assessed the verses that need further interpretation and clarification. This second source of *shari'a* are the traditions and practices of the Prophet Mohammed passed down through the centuries that complement and add further interpretation of the Quran called the Sunnah. The Sunnah derives from Hadith or the oral transmissions of the accounts, words, deeds, and practices of the Prophet Mohammed collated by scholars through the early history of Islam. These scholars developed a scientific methodology to evaluate and verify Hadith's authenticity, reliability, and trustworthiness. In what became known as *'ilm al Hadith* (the science of Hadith), scholars analyzed the chain of narration of each Hadith and scrutinized the character, piety, and intellect of the transmitters, among other criteria, to distinguish the Hadith that would be binding and those that are spurious and therefore disregarded. Around two centuries after the Prophet Mohammed's death, compilations were collected of methodologically sound Hadith. The most famous of these Hadith collections were the six books referred to as the *al sahih al sittah*, or the Authentic Six.

The subsequent two sources dealt with new jurisprudential challenges and questions the Muslim community faced during the early expansion of Islam and extended the existing rulings to these unfamiliar circumstances.

22 The Islamic Legal Tradition

Ijtihad or independent legal reasoning of qualified Islamic scholars used *ijma'* or scholarly consensus and *qiyas al fuqaha* or the analogical deduction in matters not covered in the Quran or Sunnah. The concept of *ijma'* is similar to the legal term in common law for *stare decisis* and the practice of precedent (Nyazee, 2000). The legal principle extracted its authority from Hadiths stating, "My *ummah* (community) will never agree upon an error." The participation of scholars in this collective *ijtihad* was a critical aspect of Islamic legal history since political rulers had no authority over the religious sphere, and the Muslim world did not institute a formal religious establishment to agree on interpretations.

Furthermore, the applicability of *ijma'* was onerous, had little impact on legal development, and accounted for less than 1% of classical jurisprudence (Hallaq, 2009a, p. 22). The fourth source of *shari'a* is individual scholarly *ijtihad* in *qiyas al fuqaha* or the analogical deduction by competent jurists. *Qiyas* was always positioned lower than *ijma'* as a source and was concerned with the methodology of deriving a ruling by scriptural analogy (Ramadan, 2006). According to Hallaq (2009b, p. 101), scholars first identify a new case; find an original case from the Quran, Sunnah, or *ijma'*; apply *ratio legis* (the claim of similarity between the new and original cases); and finally, transpose the legal norm in the original case to the new one.

Other scholars apply *maqasid shari'a* (objectives of *shari'a*) as a source of Islamic law. The *maqasid* is the legal doctrine that centers on *maslaha* (public interest) to understand the *shari'a*'s intent and purposes (Ibn Ashur, 1999). In the 11th century, Imam Ghazali, one of the foremost commentators on *maqasid*, argued *maslaha* was God's purpose of revealing divine law and, along with his teacher Imam Juwayni, identified five objectives in *shari'a* (Auda, 2008). These five elements became known as the *al daruriyyat al khamsa* and include the preservation of *deen* (religion), *nafs* (life), *'aql* (intellect), *nasl* (offspring), and *mal* (property) (Opwis, 2007). *Maqasid* scholars call on Muslims toward treating the religion as a "fountain of values that guide conduct" (Khan, 2003). These principal values comprise human dignity, justice, equality, freedom, universal moral values, *shura* (human representation and participation), and the rule of law (Farooq, 2013).

Within Islamic law, numerous schools of thought developed from the 8th to the 10th centuries. In the Sunni world, Imam Abu Hanifa implemented *ray* (opinion), *'urf* (custom), and *istihsan* (juristic discretion) to derive rulings. The Hanafis are the majority in the Muslim world as the Abbasids, Ottomans, and Mughals adopted the Hanafi School throughout their vast empires. Imam Malik was a judge in the city of Medina that emphasized the *'amal* (practices and customs) of the early generation of Muslims in Medina as a source along with *masalih al mursala* (public interest) *istihsan*, *'urf*, and *ad dhra'i* (facilitating or blocking the means toward an action). The Maliki school of thought is predominant in North and West Africa and across the Arabian Peninsula. Imam Shafi'i was the founder of the third school of thought and was known for codifying and advancing the field of *usul al fiqh* (principles of Islamic jurisprudence). The Imam was the first to systematize qiyas' rules and rejected *istihsan* and *istislah* (public interest) as sources. The Shafi'i school of thought spread throughout East Africa, Egypt, the Levant, Yemen, and Central and Southeast Asia. The fourth Sunni school is that of Imam Ahmad ibn Hanbal. Imam Ahmad restricted his rulings to the traditional textual sources, *ad dhra'i*, and was opposed to certain aspects of *ijma'* and *istihsan*. Out of the Sunni schools, the Hanbali has the smallest number of followers, with the majority of them concentrated in the Arabian Peninsula. As for the Shi'a, the majority follow Imam Ja'far al Sadiq's school of thought throughout Lebanon, Iraq, parts of the Arabian Gulf, Iran, and the Indian subcontinent. Smaller schools of thought like the Ibadis in Oman, the Zaydis in Yemen, and the Zahiris associated with some Salafist movements endure, while numerous others declined and became extinct (Eyadat, 2012). The rulings by these Imams were not codified into law but were recorded, disseminated, and debated in scholarly literature, with jurists extracting judgments from across the Muslim world. The various schools of thought and their methodologies categorized legal rulings into those that are *wajib* (obligatory), *mandub* (recommended), *mubah* (permissible), *makruh* (disliked), or *haram* (prohibited) (Hallaq, 1997).

In Islamic criminal law, offenses are divided into *hudud*, *qisas*, and *ta'zir*. These categories in Islamic law were established by jurists in the development of the Islamic legal system rather than the Quran (Brown, 2017, p. 5). *Hudud* is the plural for *hadd*, which means limit, border, or boundary. *Hudud* crimes and punishments are violations against the rights of God that the Quran and Sunnah predetermine with strict conditions. In *hudud* crimes, Muslim jurists identify five:

- *sariqa* (furtive theft),
- *zina* (illicit sexual relations),
- *qadhf* (defamation or unsubstantiated accusation of sexual relations),
- *shrub al khamr* (consumption of intoxicants), and
- *hiraba* (armed robbery banditry/terrorism).

Based on injunctions from the Quran and Sunnah, *hudud* are not subject to interpretation and contain mandatory prescribed punishments once an individual concludes the criminal process and is convicted. Since *hudud* were violations against the rights of God, jurists developed legal principles that reflect God's mercy in implementing *hudud* punishments called *idra'u al ḥudud bil shubuhat* (Islamic canon of doubt) or the instructions for judges on how to avoid punishment in the cases of doubt (Rabb, 2015). Throughout history, Muslim scholars encouraged the legal principle to "ward off the *hudud* by *shubuhat* (ambiguities)" (Yorke & Nazir, 2019, p. 366). Judges would actively scrutinize *shubuhat* in cases and rigorously seek restrictions that would hinder the application of a *hadd* punishment.

Qisas are crimes that cause physical bodily injury or homicide, requiring *lex taliones* (retribution). Jurists categorize these offenses as violations against the rights of humans and are settled between the victim and offender either through *qisas*, *diyya* (financial compensation), or forgiveness/reconciliation as encouraged by the Quran (Hascall, 2011). Those cases that are not categorized under *qisas* or are precluded from *hudud* are placed in the *ta'zir* category. *Ta'zir* are discretionary punishments for crimes not set in the Quran or Sunnah for particular sins or actions that undermine the community or threaten the public order (Burns, 2014). In the cases of *ta'zir*, the state or *qadi* (judge) is authorized to exercise judicial discretion. In the classical Islamic legal system, the *qadi* is in charge of the court, and a mufti is a legal scholar that provides counseling in Islamic affairs, elaborates on laws, advises the courts, and issues fatwas (Masud & Kéchichian, 2009). The ascertainment of truth, determination of the responsibility, and the remedies to the victim and societies were the purposes and goals of the *qadi*, courts, and the administration of criminal justice (Bassiouni, 1982, p. 24).

The study of Arab criminology requires basic knowledge of the manifold schools of thought and the historical development of the diversified practices and variations of Islamic law across the Arab world. For many Muslims, there is a favorable perception of Islamic law. Ibn al Qayyim, a 14th-century scholar, once proclaimed that Islamic law

> is all about justice, mercy, wisdom, and good. Thus, any ruling that replaces justice with injustice, mercy with its opposite, common good with mischief, or wisdom with nonsense, is a ruling that does not belong to the Islamic law, even if it is claimed to be so according to some interpretation.
> (Ibn al Qayyim, 1973, p. 333; in Auda, 2008, p. 21)

Fiqh prevailed as a scholarly endeavor that presented shifting interpretations within and between the various schools of thought. Nevertheless, the Islamic legal tradition transformed entirely with European exploration and colonization of the Arab world.

Colonialism and Legal Importation

Despite the stereotypes, Islamic law has traditionally been flexible in its application, as demonstrated by the various dynasties, empires, and kingdoms throughout history. At its zenith, the Muslim and Arab world achieved a legacy that influenced many academic fields and disciplines (Al-Khalili, 2011; Renima et al., 2016). In medieval Europe, Islamic law originated the 12-member jury system and developed the English trust and agency institutions and the assize of novel disseisin for the common law tradition (Gaudiosi, 1988; Makdisi, 1999). Other European nations of the civil law tradition adopted the legal concepts of *hawala, qirad*, and *mudaraba* (Badr, 1978; Boisard, 1980; Çizakça, 2014). Al Qarawiyyin in Fes, Al Azhar in Cairo, and Mustansiriya Madrasah in Baghdad along with and many other legal institutions produced myriad scholars, jurists, and *qadis* for over a millennium. Scholars such as Al Shaybani in the 8th century wrote multiple volumes on international law (Bashir, 2018), while others like the polymath Ibn Rushd (Averroes) reintroduced Aristotle to the West and contributed the treatise *bidayat al mujtahid* to the field of *fiqh*. The rise of the Ottomans brought many parts of the Arab world to the Ottoman Caliphate's Hanafi *Kanun* and *millet* systems (Hathaway, 2019). The drastic transformation of Arab legal systems occurred in the 19th and 20th centuries during conquests by the French, British, Spanish, and Italian empires, as Huntington (1996) pointed out: "the West won the world not by the superiority of its ideas or values or religion but rather by its superiority in applying organized violence" (51). By 1800, Western colonial powers controlled 35% of the earth's surface, 67% by 1874, and 85% by 1914 (Said, 2012).

Simultaneous with the rise of modern nation-states, the West deemed Arab societies as uncivilized, irrational, and less enlightened. Orientalism, the process that propagandized colonization, was a pivotal instrument in restructuring the Islamic legal and criminal justice systems. Said (1978) argues that Orientalism rationalized the policies and conditions for the West to undertake the colonial project. The generated perceptions of Islamic law illustrate the concept of legal orientalism or the impression of a lawless orient whose legal system underperforms compared to European traditions (Ruskola, 2013). Orientalist campaigns of disinformation targeted Islamic scholars and institutions with the myth that they had closed all doors of *ijtihad*. Orientalists convinced the Arab and Muslim world that Islamic law had stopped developing 1,000 years ago, and people were now practicing *taqlid* (blind imitation) of the law (Abou el Fadl, 2014). Since the Islamic legal system impeded the commercial and economic interests of the colonial powers, the transposition of *shari'a* courts became a priority. These and other accusations effectively justified the restriction and eventual replacement of Islamic law by European legal codes and a state-controlled rather than an uncodified jurist-controlled legal system. The colonial powers first established state government courts that coexisted with Islamic courts. Eventually, the state supplanted Islamic courts with state courts that implemented unfamiliar European legal norms and values. Instead of citizens presenting their cases to *qadis*, Western-educated professional lawyers disputed cases in hybrid courts that mixed legal traditions. Throughout the 20th century, the European civil court system replaced the Islamic courts and relegated *sharia'* to family or personal status laws.

One segment of essential participants in this transformation were the native elites that maneuvered parasitically against their citizens to procure the benefits provided by colonial powers (Abou el Fadl, 2014). When Europeans repudiated the local Islamic laws, the Arab elites compromised the deep-rooted institutions to preserve their privileged status. One realm that solidified the elites' hegemony and further disintegrated the practice of Islamic law was the colonial educational system. Western universities and academic institutions became one of the few paths toward social mobility and access to opportunities. The requirement of Western education for various government jobs rendered the study of *sharia'* disadvantageous and deprived Muslim jurists of any state authority. As the legal importation of European models was nearly complete, the new systems excluded Islamic scholars from political roles and severely undermined their legitimacy. Even more destructive were the epistemological attacks on Islamic jurisprudence and thought that proliferated unorthodox interpretations and deviated from classical *fiqh* (Sabic-El-Rayess, 2020).

The Arab states inherited an array of mixed legal systems, evoking the implanted projects that fulfilled colonial interests (Provence, 2008; Hoffman, 2010). These colonial administrations were initially designed to maintain political and economic interests and continued into the postcolonial governments. Post-independence regimes that sustained these systems were incongruous with Islamic jurisprudence. The police, courts, and prisons replicated the highly centralized colonial structures that led directly to the Ministry of the Interior or the head of state. In some Arab governments, *sharia'* persisted as an inspiration and additional source of law (Crystal, 2001; Brown, 2017a). While most of the Arab world adopted a mixture of Islamic and European (usually French) legal systems, others, including Qatar and Saudi Arabia, never replaced their *sharia'*-based legal systems (Peters, 2005). Meanwhile, others became inspired by distinct political philosophies of Third Worldism, Ba'athism, Islamism, or, in Algeria's case, socialist-Islamic legal principles (Hazard, 1981). Since the Cold War split between the Western-backed monarchies and Soviet-backed republics, numerous governments, regimes, and movements reintroduced and readopted Islamic law in manifold variations throughout the Arab world (Kramer, 2017).

Islamic Law and Arab Criminology

Since the Iranian Revolution, the Taliban takeover of Afghanistan in the 1990s, and the proliferation of terrorist organizations after the 9/11 attacks, many people have surmised Islamic law as a rigid and regressive legal code appropriate only for medieval societies. Others recognize the position of *sharia'* for Muslims but perceive Islamic law as deficient in its modern application and only tolerate its practice in private and not in public matters. There are several reasons for these present-day perceptions of Islamic law.

One factor is the hostile escalation in Islamophobia since the attacks on 9/11. For example, in the United States, several states prohibited *sharia'* law despite the lack of a definition of what *sharia'* is and having no history of any adversities with Islamic laws or Muslim communities (Berger, 2018). The Islamophobia industry has now become a multimillion-dollar business in misrepresenting Arab culture and Islam to the public in what has become known as the "green scare" (Ekman, 2015; Abadi, 2018). The media has become an integral reason for the persistent inaccurate and harmful depictions of Islam and Muslims in the media (Ahmed & Matthes, 2017). News coverage often portrays Arabs and Muslims as erratic, aggressive, and incompatible with the norms of the international community. Media exposure to these negative portrayals increases stereotypes to the point that participants in numerous studies on Islamophobia believe Muslims are always behind terrorist attacks (Schmuck et al., 2018), should have their civil rights restricted, and support military action against countries located in the Arab/Muslim world (Saleem et al., 2017). These exacerbated negative representations benefit the military–industrial complex and can be lucrative for unscrupulous governments. The wars in Afghanistan and Iraq and countless drone attacks on Somalia, Yemen, Syria, Libya, and others in the War on Terror necessitate Orientalism, Islamophobia, and anti-Arab racism to justify military force (Salaita, 2006). These opportune depictions of the Arab world revive the colonial strategies of the past that now contribute to neocolonial policies (Nkrumah, 1965).

An unfortunate aspect of these destructive representations is the perverse applications of Islamic law by extremists and terrorist organizations that reinforce the characterizations presented by Orientalists and Islamophobes. Groups like *Daesh* or ISIS (the Islamic State of Iraq and Syria) that reduce the *sharia'* to "obscurantist confinement, medieval stubbornness, and fanaticism" (Ramadan, 2001, p. 47) are an affront to the intellectual legacy of *fiqh*. The zeal for reestablishing Islamic law by specific Islamic movements and groups often overlooks the contributions of *maqasid*, *maslaha/mafsada*, *shubuhat*, and the essence of justice within the Islamic legal tradition. Rather than a simple litmus test on whether there is an enforcement of *huddud*, an Islamic system must develop an effective system of dealing with poverty, illiteracy, authoritarianism, political violence, and economic instability required by *shari'a*. Muslims must cherish the contributions of the past and look forward to future challenges.

In contemporary criminal justice, the Islamic legal tradition manifests in several forms. Each Arab nation's criminal justice system has adopted various Islamic legal principles to different degrees. In the United Arab Emirates, the judiciary consists of civil, criminal, and *shari'a* courts. The *shari'a* courts have jurisdiction over family and criminal laws (Kamali, 2019). Morocco's interpretations of the Maliki school rely on the flexibility of *'urf* and *maslaha*. The existence of *'urf* allows for a more adaptive and informal approach to dispute resolution practiced outside of the rigidity of a formal court system (Hanafi, 2020). A vital contribution of Islamic law is the concepts of *sulh* (amicable settlement) and *musalaha* (reconciliation) (Irani & Funk, 1998). *Sulh* and *musalaha* are instrumental for the various truth and reconciliation commissions, pardons, clemencies, amnesties, and other conflict resolutions in post-conflict Arab societies (Ghosn, 2018; Zartman, 2020; Ouassini, 2022).

This chapter attempts to demonstrate how a sub-discipline of Arab criminology requires an intimate knowledge of the development of Islamic thought from the time of the Prophet Mohammed until the 21st century and across a vast array of cultures, empires, and geographies in the Arab and Muslim world. The chapter introduced the reader to the differences between *shari'a* and *fiqh*, the sources of Islamic law, the four schools of Islamic thought, and the *hadd*, *qisas*, and *ta'zir* categories of Islamic criminal laws and punishment. Currently, there are many distorted perceptions of Islamic law, a consequence of long-standing misinformation from Orientalists. The decline of Islamic law in the Arab world occurred during the movement of legal importation brought about by colonialism that formed Eurocentric systems that became spheres of legal experimentation (Dupret et al., 1999), severing Islamic scholars from *fiqh*, and transferring the craft of law-making to the aristocracy and the state. These events displaced the entire history and legal culture that existed before colonialism in the Arab world.

As a result of inheriting direct control over the legal sphere from their former colonial powers, many Arab governments continue to confine Islamic law to the margins of family and personal status laws. Unlike the autonomous scholars in the pre-colonial era, the state determines the contents of the law and revises the aspects of *shari'a* considered a threat or not congruent with its objectives. The state has deviated from the traditional *fiqh* by applying *talfiq* (blending the rulings derived from various methodologies and schools into one) for rules and interpretations it deems advantageous to the state. Rather than the pre-colonial universality of the schools of thought, states now claim to be Islamic in their use of *fiqh*, whose system might ultimately differ from one nation to another in unrecognizable variations due to the practice of blending in *talfiq*. To the Arab states, Islamic law is pertinent to its legitimacy and control of the religious narrative. Unlike other legal traditions, Islamic law's merging of morality and law makes it communally focused, legitimate, and less coercive and empowers the system by gaining the public's deference, obedience, and cooperation (Tyler, 2003; Hallaq, 2009b).

For Arab criminology, the chapter highlights the role of Islamic law in shaping the cultural, legal, and political definitions of crime and punishment in the Arab world. The function of religion in Arab legal systems requires knowledge of the intersecting realities of law, crime, justice, and religion (Bassiouni, 2014; Nassery et al., 2018). Despite the history of Orientalism, the current trends in Islamophobia, and neocolonial policies in the region, the study of *shari'a* and the various interpretations of *fiqh* is a necessary component of Arab criminology. *Shari'a* will continue to be a contested topic. Still, there is no doubt that the Islamic religion is a powerful force guiding the thinking, behavior, conduct, and reaction to criminal justice issues. This chapter encourages the reader to explore the topic of Islamic law in the Arab world further and argues categorically that an Arab criminology sub-discipline is more suitable to examine and appreciate the nuanced role of Islam in Arab legal and criminal justice systems than the current approaches in Northern criminology.

References

Abadi, H. (2018). *Countering the Islamophobia industry: Toward more effective strategies*. The Carter Center.
Abdal-Haqq, I. (2002). Islamic law: An overview and its elements. *Journal of Islamic Law and Culture*, 27(7).
Abou El Fadl, K. (2014). *Reasoning with god: Reclaiming Shari'ah in the modern age*. Rowman & Littlefield.
Ahmed, S., & Matthes, J. (2017). Media representation of Muslims and Islam from 2000 to 2015: A meta-analysis. *International Communication Gazette*, 79(3), 219–244.
Al-Khalili, J. (2011). *The house of wisdom: How Arabic science saved ancient knowledge and gave us the Renaissance*. Penguin.
Auda, J. (2008). *Maqasid al-Shariah as philosophy of Islamic law: A systems approach*. International Institute of Islamic Thought (IIIT).
Baderin, M. A. (2005). *International Human Rights and Islamic law* (pp. 32–40). Oxford University Press.

Badr, G. M. (1978). Islamic law: Its relations to other legal systems. *American Journal of Comparative Law*, *26*, 187–198.
Bashir, K. R. (2018). *Islamic International Law: Historical foundations and Al-Shaybani's Siyar*. Edward Elgar Publishing.
Bassiouni, M. C. (1982). Sources of Islamic law, and the protection of human rights in the Islamic criminal justice system. In M. C. Bassiouni (Ed.), *The Islamic criminal system*. (pp. 3–53). Oceana Publications.
Bassiouni, M. C. (2014). *The Shari'a and Islamic criminal justice in time of war and peace*. Cambridge University Press.
Berger, M. S. (2018). Understanding sharia in the west. *Journal of Law, Religion and State*, *6*(2–3), 236–273.
Boisard, M. A. (1980). On the probable influence of Islam on western public and international law. *International Journal of Middle East Studies*, *11*(4), 429–450.
Brown, D. W. (2017a). *A new introduction to Islam*. John Wiley & Sons.
Brown, J. (2017b). *Official Islam in the Arab world: The contest for religious authority*. Carnegie Endowment for International Peace. https://carnegieendowment.org/2017/05/11/official-islam-in-arab-world-contest-for-religious-authority-pub-6992
Brown, J. (2017c, January 12). Stoning and hand cutting – Understanding the Hudud and the Shariah in Islam. *Yaqeen Institute*. https://yaqeeninstitute.org/en/jonathan-brown/stoning-and-handcutting-understanding-the-hudud-and-the-shariah-in-islam/
Burns, J. G. (2014). *Introduction to Islamic law: Principles of civil, criminal, and international law under the Shari'a*. Teller Books.
Çizakça, M. (2014). Risk sharing and risk shifting: An historical perspective. *Borsa Istanbul Review*, *14*(4), 191–195.
Cross, C. (2018). Marginalized voices: The absence of Nigerian scholars in global examinations of online fraud. In K. Carrington, R. Hogg, J. Scott, & M. Sozzo (Eds.), *The Palgrave handbook of criminology and the global south* (pp. 261–280). Palgrave Macmillan.
Crystal, J. (2001). Criminal justice in the Middle East. *Journal of Criminal Justice*, *29*, 469–482.
Doi, A. (1984) *Shari'ah: The Islamic law*. Ta-Ha Publishers.
Dupret, B., Berger, M., & Al-Zwaini, L. (Eds.). (1999). *Legal pluralism in the Arab world*. Kluwer Law International.
Ekman, M. (2015). Online Islamophobia and the politics of fear: Manufacturing the green scare. *Ethnic and Racial Studies*, *38*(11), 1986–2002.
Eyadat, Z. (2012). Islams: Between dialoguing and mainstreaming. *Philosophy & Social Criticism*, *38*(4–5), 507–516.
Farooq, M. O. (2013). *Toward our reformation: From legalism to value-oriented Islamic law and jurisprudence*. International Institute of Islamic Thought.
Gaudiosi, M. (1988). The influence of the Islamic law of waqf on the development of the Trust in England: The case of Merton College. *University of Pennsylvania Law Review*, *136*(4), 1231–1261.
Ghosn, F. (2018). The hard road ahead for Syrian reconstruction. *Current History*, *117*(803), 331–337.

Greer, T. H. (1987). *A brief history of the western world*. New York: Harcourt Brace Jovsanovich Publishers.
Hallaq, W. B. (1997). *A history of Islamic legal theories: An introduction to Sunni Usul al-Fiqh*. Cambridge University Press.
Hallaq, W. B. (2009b). *Sharī'a: Theory, practice, transformations*. Cambridge University Press.
Hallaq, W. B. (2009a). *An introduction to Islamic law*. Cambridge University Press.
Hanafi, L. (2020). The legal system of Morocco. *Comparative Studies in Society and History*, *52*(4), 851–880.
Hascall, S. C. (2011). Restorative justice in Islam: Should Qisas be considered a form of restorative justice. *Berkeley Journal of Middle Eastern & Islamic Law*, *4*(1), 35–78.
Hathaway, J. (2019). *The Arab lands under Ottoman rule: 1516–1800*. Routledge.
Hazard, J. N. (1981). Socialism and law in Algeria. *Review of Socialist Law*, *3*(7), 243–260.
Hoffman, K. E. (2010). Berber law by French means: Customary courts in the Moroccan hinterlands, 1930–1956. *Comparative Studies in Society and History*, *52*, 851–880.
Huntington, S. P. (1996). *The clash of civilizations and the remaking of world order*. Simon & Schuster.
Ibn al-Qayyim, S. (1973). *I'lam al-Muwaqqi'in* (Vol. 1., Ed. T. A. R. Saad). Dar al-Jil.
Ibn Ashur, M. T. (1999). *Maqasid al-Shari'ah al-Islamiyyah*. Ed. el-Tahir el-Mesawi. al-Fajr.
Irani, G. E., & Funk, N. C. (1998). Rituals of reconciliation: Arab-Islamic perspectives. *Arab Studies Quarterly*, 53–73.
Kamali, M. H. (2008). *Shari'ah law: An introduction*. Oneworld Publications.
Kamali, M. H. (2019). *Crime and punishment in Islamic law: A fresh interpretation*. Oxford University Press.
Khan, M. (2003, April). The Priority of Politics: A Response to 'Islam and the Challenge of Democracy.' *Boston Review*. http://bostonreview.net/BR28.2/khan.html.
Kramer, M. (2017). *Arab awakening and Islamic revival: The politics of ideas in the Middle East*. Routledge.
Makdisi, J. A. (1999). The Islamic origins of the common law. *North Carolina Law Review*, *77*(5), 1635–1739.
Masud, M. K., & Kéchichian, J. A. (2009). Fatwā. Concepts of Fatwā. In J. L. Esposito (Ed.), *The Oxford encyclopedia of the Islamic world*. Oxford University Press.
Moosavi, L. (2018). Decolonising criminology: Syed Hussein Alatas on crimes of the powerful. *Critical Criminology*, 1–14.
Nassery, I., Ahmed, R., & Tatari, M. (Eds.). (2018). *The objectives of Islamic law: The promises and challenges of the Maqāṣid Al-sharī'a*. Lexington Books.
Nkrumah, K. (1965). *Neo-colonialism: The last stage of imperialism*. Nelson.
Nyazee, I. A. K. (2000). *Islamic jurisprudence (Usul al fiqh)*. International Institute of Islamic Thought.
Opwis, F. (2007). Islamic law and legal change: The concept of Maslaha in classical and contemporary Islamic legal theory. In A. Abbas & F. Griffel (Eds.), *Shari'a: Islamic law in the contemporary context* (pp. 62–82). Stanford University Press.

Ouassini, N. (2022). North Africa's truth and reconciliation commissions and transitional justice in the Maghreb. In S. Sungi & N. Ouassini (Eds.), *Comparative criminology across western and African perspectives* (pp. 180–194). IGI Global.

Ouassini, N., & Ouassini, A. (2020). Criminology in the Arab world: Misconceptions, nuances and future prospects. *The British Journal of Criminology*, *60*(3), 519–536.

Peters, R. (2005). *Crime and punishment in Islamic Law: Theory and practice from the sixteenth to the twenty-first century (No. 2)*. Cambridge University Press.

Provence, M. (2008). "Liberal colonialism" and martial law in French mandate Syria. In C. Schumann (Ed.), *Liberal thought in the eastern Mediterranean: Late nineteenth century until the 1960s*. Brill.

Rabb, I. A. (2015). *Doubt in Islamic law*. Cambridge University Press.

Ramadan, H. M. (Ed.). (2006). *Understanding Islamic law: From classical to contemporary*. AltaMira Press.

Ramadan, T. (2001). *Islam, the west and the challenges of modernity*. The Islamic Foundation.

Renima, A., Tiliouine, H., & Estes, R. J. (2016). The Islamic golden age: A story of the triumph of the Islamic civilization. In H. Tiliouine &, R. Estes (Eds.), *The state of social progress of Islamic societies. International handbooks of quality-of-life*. Springer.

Robinson, F. (1982). *Atlas of the Islamic world since 1500*. Facts on File.

Ruskola, T. (2013). *Legal orientalism*. Harvard University Press.

Sabic-El-Rayess, A. (2020). Epistemological shifts in knowledge and education in Islam: A new perspective on the emergence of radicalization amongst Muslims. *International Journal of Educational Development*, *73*, 102148.

Said, E. (1978). *Orientalism*. Vintage Books.

Said, E. (2012). *Culture and imperialism*. Vintage.

Salaita, S. (2006). Beyond orientalism and Islamophobia: 9/11, anti-Arab racism, and the mythos of national pride. *The New Centennial Review*, *6*(2), 245–266.

Saleem, M., Prot, S., Anderson, C. A., & Lemieux, A. F. (2017). Exposure to Muslims in media and support for public policies harming Muslims. *Communication Research*, *44*(6), 841–869.

Schmuck, D., Matthes, J., von Sikorski, C., Materne, N., & Shah, E. (2018). Are unidentified terrorist suspects always Muslims? How terrorism news shape news consumers' automatic activation of Muslims as perpetrators. *Religions*, *9*(10), 286. http://dx.doi.org/10.3390/rel9100286

Tyler, T. R. (2003). Procedural justice, legitimacy, and the effective rule of law. *Crime and justice*, *30*, 283–357.

Yorke, J., & Nazir, A. (2019). Imagining Utopia: The global abolition of the death penalty. In C. S. Steiker & J. M. Steiker (Eds.), *Comparative capital punishment* (pp. 341–370). Edward Elgar Publishing.

Zartman, J. K. (2020). Development and peace through traditional, cultural, Islamic mediation. *Journal of Peacebuilding & Development*, *15*(2), 164–177.

3 Historical, Political, and Cultural Commonalities

Introduction

History, politics, and culture are indispensable variables in analyzing crime and criminal justice in the Arab world. Unlike other regions in international and comparative criminologies, Arab countries conspicuously share similar "language, ethnicity, history, customs, and political aspirations" (Choueiri, 2000, p. 91), as explicitly expressed in the 1945 founding of the Arab League. Headquartered in Cairo, the Arab League initially consisted of Iraq, Lebanon, Saudi Arabia, Syria, Transjordan, and Yemen and has since expanded to 22 states with more than 400 million citizens. In the post-colonial world, Arab states bolstered their support for the League to safeguard their independence and sovereignty and to collaborate with other Arab states in politics, economics, communications, culture, social welfare, health, crime and security, as well as other cooperative matters (Pact of the League of Arab States, Article 1 & 2). Currently, the League includes Algeria, Bahrain, Comoros, Djibouti, Egypt, Iraq, Jordan, Kuwait, Lebanon, Libya, Mauritania, Morocco, Oman, Palestine, Qatar, Saudi Arabia, Somalia, Sudan, Syria, Tunisia, United Arab Emirates, and Yemen. All the listed countries self-identify with the geopolitical map of *al watan al 'arabi* (the Arab homeland). One of the key features of membership in the Arab League has been pronounced through its application of a broad-based linguistic definition of Arab identity to include any "person whose language is Arabic, who lives in an Arabic speaking country, and who is in sympathy with the aspirations of the Arabic speaking people" (Albirini, 2020, p. 176).

The Arab League's comprehensive definition consolidates Arab identity around linguistic and historical terms while positioning racial, ethnic, and religious frameworks as secondary. This is central to the underlying logic formulating the disciplinary boundaries of Arab criminology. These concepts of Arab identity originated in the *Nahda* (Renaissance) Movement in the late 19th century, when thinkers such as Sati Al-Husri argued that race was an unreliable representation of the various origins of the Arab people

(Choueiri, 2000). According to Suleiman (1994), Al-Husri theorized that the Arab language and history are the primary principles of Arab nationalism. By borrowing from German nationalist ideologies, Al-Husri declared the Arabic language to be the guardian of cultural heritage, its religion, traditions, music, poetry, and folklore preserved and passed down from generation to generation. Language is then "the medium and substance of cultural delivery," more valuable than territory and the guarantor of cultural continuity and permanence, especially in the face of colonialism (Suleiman, 1994, pp. 13–14). Zaki al Arsuzi, Michel Aflaq, Abdullah al Alayli, and other writers from the period also emphasized a linguistic identity and rejected racial constructs that would partition the Arab nation, undermine its grand objectives, and advance the interests of Western imperial powers (Elgawly, 2017). As Albert Hourani, the renowned Arabist, comments,

> For better or worse, this [linguistic nationalism] became the dominant political idea in the Middle East and superseded or absorbed the others; thus, in the Arabic-speaking countries, the assertion that all who speak Arabic formed a nation and should constitute one State or group of States proved to be the strongest political force.
>
> (cited in Bitar, 2011, p. 52)

This conceptualization of the Arab homeland produced various diverging ideologies, often upholding state-centric policies above any pan-Arab priorities to unify (Mabry, 2015). Eventually, the Arab League became an inefficacious alliance between self-identified Arab states, each seeking interests in an organization that lacked a process to compel members to abide by its resolutions. The decade after the Arab Spring, the Arab League had a majority vote to freeze membership for Libya and Syria. These were the first suspensions of member states for domestic issues (Egypt was suspended for its peace treaty with Israel in 1979). Debre (2021) asserts that these policies were an effort toward survival politics to re-legitimize and preserve member states' authoritarian rule. Toward their own citizens, these states were signaling their supposed understanding of public grievances without a genuine commitment to reform. As a result, many citizens of the Arab world have suspended any hope in an organization known in the region as a "glorified debating society" (Masters & Sergie, 2020) rather than a resolute alliance formed to advance the region toward the future. However, the resiliency of pan-Arabism and the idea of the Arab league remain.

Deficiencies riddle the linguistic conceptualization of the Arab identity. The Arab world is a multifaceted region with diverse races, ethnicities, cultures, religions, and languages. Most Arab states consist of distinct ethnicities that only exist within their borders as Arabic-speaking citizens, closely sympathizing with the aspirations of Arabic people, but would not identify as Arab. The Amazigh (Berbers), Coptic, Kurdish, Somali, and other ethnic groups have a complex relationship with Arab history, politics, and cultures. The coexistence between the various cultures in the Arab world has complicated the conceptualization of Arab linguistic identity, exemplified by the diglossia in Arabic dialects. Every Arab nation has its colloquial language known as *darija* or *'ammiyya*, often influenced by the local or regional ethnic groups, cultures, and history. For example, Moroccan Arabic is a dialect that many in the Arab world have difficulty understanding due to its extensive Amazigh (Berber) influence, with certain loanwords from French and Spanish reflecting its rich history. Nevertheless, Modern Standard Arabic (MSA) has become the official standard used in academia, literature, media, government, and other formal forms of communication across the Arab world and is the lingua franca of Arab academia. Despite the limitations associated with the Arab League's linguistic approach to Arab identity, the intersection between the region's collective history, political systems in the post-colonial world, and commonalities in language and culture advance a cogent argument for Arab criminology when compared to other geographical-related criminologies.

This chapter will examine and substantiate the assertion that the mutuality of Arab historical, political, and cultural ties provides the sub-discipline a foundation for critically understanding crime and criminal justice in the region. The chapter will introduce the reader to Arab history, postulating the region's experiences from the expansion of Islam to post-colonial era corroborates the establishment of an Arab criminological sub-discipline. The next section will assess the political conditions in the Arab world as a second commonality. Finally, the chapter will discuss the centrality of culture among and between contemporary Arab nations with a specific focus on Arab media.

A Collective History

The collective history of the Arab world reveals "how traces of the past – in material and memorial forms, both within particular institutions and amongst the population at large – persist in the present, and the role these traces play in contemporary (Arab) crime and justice" (Churchill, 2017, p. 8). Before the advent of Islam, the Arab people predominantly inhabited the Arabian Peninsula. The linguistic distinction grounded Arab ethnogenesis between the *'arab* or those that communicate clearly in *lughat daad* (the language of daad, a letter unique to the Arabic language) as opposed to those the Arabs called the *'ajam* or those that are incapable of communicating articulately, that is, non-Arabic speakers. As a Semitic language, Arabic belongs to the family of Amharic, Aramaic, Hebrew, and Syriac, among others. Originally the Arabs were divided into three categories; *al 'arab al ba'ida* (perished Arabs), *al 'arab al 'ariba* (pure Arabs), and *al 'arab al musta'riba* (Arabized Arabs) (Mahoney, 2016, p. 169). Aside from sharing a common language, the pre-Islamic Arabs identified with tribal and regional affiliations and were too fragmented to unite (Webb, 2016). The tribes lacked a definitive political structure or collective religious affiliation and faced relentless tribal feuds like the notorious pre-Islamic wars of *al basous* and *al fijar*.

The Prophet Mohammed's mission, the Quran, and the emergence of Islam unified the Arabs and, according to Webb (2016), were the impetus for Arab ethnogenesis that evolved through the subsequent centuries of scholars and dynasties. Islam's early denouncement of racial, ethnic, and tribal chasms actualized a cohesive Arab identity. The focus on Quranic Arabic as the lingua franca and the ascendance of Islam as a unifying creed open for converts bonded the Arab people in expanding through vast geographical areas. Under *al khulafa' ar Rashidun*, or the first four Caliphs after the Prophet Mohammed's death, the Arabs had subdued all regional powers: the Romans/Byzantines and Sassanids in Syria, Persia, Armenia, Egypt, and Cyprus. Among Arab nationalists, the Islamic expansion is an Arab milestone, a sentiment echoed by members of the Nahda Movement in the 19th and 20th centuries. The contributions of the Islamic civilization have become synonymic with the Arab world; Sulaiman (2007) explains, "To most of the Arabs, Islam is their indigenous religion; to all of the Arabs, Islam is their indigenous civilization." Even Christian Arabs described Islam and the role of the Prophet Mohammed as integral to Arab nationalism (Helms, 1990; Choueiri, 2000), often borrowing rhetoric and expressions directly from the Quran (Halliday, 2013).

By the Umayyad dynasty, Islam had spread from the Iberian Peninsula in the west to Sindh in the east. Unlike the first four Caliphs, the Banu Umayyah deviated from the *shura* (community consultation) approach toward the Caliphate and into hereditary kingships requiring absolute obedience to the sovereign (Lohlker, 2016). Although the Umayyads expanded Islamic rule, they enforced discriminatory policies that accelerated their end. To integrate the *mawali* (non-Arab Muslims), the Umayyads imposed a patron-client system compelling the *mawali* to declare loyalty to an Arab tribe in return for protection and support (Blankinship, 1994). The *mawali's* experiences as second-class citizens, the unjust treatment of non-Muslims in their territories, internal religious conflict, and the ineptitude in governance contributed to the downfall of the Umayyads (El-Azhari, 2019). The conquering Abbasids were far more tolerant in their interactions with the *mawali* and non-Muslims than their Damascene predecessors. The Abbasid period promoted Arab culture and the Arabic language as the language of knowledge ushering in the Islamic Golden Age. The movement to translate Greek, Roman, Persian, and Sanskrit books and the inauguration of the House of Wisdom in the Abbasid capital of Baghdad during the reign of Harun al Rashid was a historic period often highlighted by Arab nationalists (Renima et al., 2016). Nevertheless, the Abbasids fragmented into several empires: the Idrissids in Morocco, Aghalbids in Tunisia, Samanids in Central Asia, parts of modern-day Iran and Afghanistan to the Saffarids, the Fatimids in Egypt, and the last surviving member of the Umayyads establishing a Caliphate in Andalusia. The Abbasid Empire ended with Hulagu Khan's destruction of Baghdad, and their descendants were confined to ceremonial positions by the Mamluks in Egypt.

Toward the end of the Crusades and the Iberian Reconquista, the Ottomans were next to have an ever-lasting impact on the Arab world. For centuries, many Arabs were indifferent to Ottoman rule, embracing their roles as Muslim citizens of a pluralistic empire and beneficiaries of the Caliph and Defender of the Holy Cities (Kramer, 1993). Under Ottoman rule, Arab lands avoided European encroachment, particularly around the Mediterranean. The Arabs, unlike other nations under Ottoman rule, perceived themselves as "collaborators in the imperial project" rather than "subject people of the empire" (Masters, 2013, p. 7). By the time Napoleon invaded Egypt in 1798, Ottoman power was rapidly declining, and European powers were prepared to dismantle the empire that extended across three continents. As a result, the French, British, Spanish, and Italian invaded and colonized North Africa and the Middle East.

Arab nationalism originated in the challenges and amplification of Turkification and Zionism that compelled a united response (Kramer, 1993). Once the Young Turks assumed power, the policies of Turkification reoriented political sentiment from the Ottoman Empire to Turkish nationalism. The new regime often suppressed the Arabic language and instituted Turkish in government and public offices in most Arabic-speaking regions of the Ottoman empire (Suleiman, 2004). In return, Arabs responded by reasserting the Arabic language and demanded equality by initiating the Arab Revolt against Turkish rule amidst the instigation of European colonial powers. With British support, Sharif Hussein Bin Ali intended to create a state that stretched from Syria to Yemen by revolting against the Ottomans. However, when the Ottoman's alliance with the Central Powers of World War I led to their decisive defeat, Britain and France had already signed a secret treaty called the Sykes–Picot Agreement. Sykes–Picot partitioned the Middle East into arbitrary British and French mandates, shattering the British promise of an Arab state.

After the Sykes–Picot Agreement, the British openly announced the Balfour Declaration, providing a Zionist vision for a national Jewish homeland in Palestine. After the Arab Revolt, the British denied the Arabs an independent state and instead declared a new Jewish nation at their expense. In the subsequent decades, Jewish immigration into Palestine accelerated. By World War II, Zionist paramilitary and terrorist organizations, through violent acts such as the King David Hotel bombing and massacre in Deir Yassin, forced the British out of Palestine, handing the mandate back to the United Nations. The eventual United Nations Partition Plan for Palestine led to the 1948 declaration of independence for the state of Israel. For Palestinians, the plan ensured the destruction of villages, the displacement of over 750,000 Palestinians, and the loss of the vast majority of territory in Mandatory Palestine in what eventually became known as the Nakba or 'catastrophe'. These events accelerated Arab nationalism as they fully embraced and implemented Western ideas of nationalism to free themselves from European dominance and humiliation (Tibi, 1997).

In the decades following World War II, Arab nations struggled to attain independence. The most violent conflict occurred in Algeria, a nation the French had invaded in 1830 through numerous massacres, famines, rape, torture, deportations, and the extermination of around one-third of the population (Kiernan, 2008). Departmentalized in 1848, Algeria was deemed a French province, with Pied-noirs or European settlers comprising around 10% of the population. By the 1950s, Algerian nationalist groups adopted guerilla warfare to end French occupation. The French responded with torture, waterboarding, burns, rape, electroshock, slaughter, and other forms of excessive violence (Alleg, 2006). Against a nuclear power that tested and detonated more than a dozen nuclear bombs in the Sahara Desert, the Algerian struggle for independence required the support of neighboring Morocco, Tunisia, Cairo, and the Arab League. In 1962, Algeria finally gained independence after the death of over a million Algerians (Alistair, 2012). Ultimately every other Arab country gained independence, with the last remnants of European colonialization lasting until the 1970s (Bahrain, Comoros, Djibouti, Qatar, and the United Arab Emirates).

Historical enquiry and frameworks are an integral component of Arab criminology. To better understand the development of Arab criminology, scholars must be cognizant of the region's interconnected history and how criminological knowledge is produced under pre-colonial, colonial, and post-colonial contexts. A tertiary history of Arab criminology will reveal that it has a deep tradition within Islamic empires and their associated ontological and epistemological orientations, which are best represented in classical Islamic philosophy, theology, and jurisprudence. This scholarship includes classical Islamic philosophers like Ibn Khaldun, Ibn Rushd, al Ghazzali, and many other intellectuals who wrote volumes on crime, law, and criminal justice systems and processes that reflected the diverse ethnic, cultural, and political identities of the said period. However, the impact of colonization and post-colonialism has also reinforced the importance of this collective history as the modern Arab state has primarily integrated, engaged, and experimented with Northern approaches at the state and societal levels. Ultimately, the contemporary criminal justice systems in the Arab world are a result of the centuries-old integration of varied Arab and non-Arab historical epochs that include contemporary Northern and Southern approaches.

Arab Political Systems

Mahmood Mamdani (2018) contends that colonialism's principal legacy is the vestigial power structures hindering democracy. In the era of decolonization, none of the newly independent Arab states established democracy. Instead, Arab governments preserved stratified colonial administrations, institutions, and bureaucracies to sustain the status quo and serve the interests of the political elites. Harik (2006, pp. 23–24) classified post-independent Arab nations into (1) the imam–chief system, (2) the alliance system of chiefs and imams, (3) the traditional secular system, (4) the bureaucratic–military oligarchy type, and (5) the colonially created system of governments. Rulers in each classification further accelerated neo-colonial dependence in renewed political, cultural, and economic ties with the Global North, severing Arab states into either the U.S.-backed Arab monarchies or the Soviet-backed Arab republics. In the subsequent decades, pan-Arabism and Islamic movements unequivocally opposed neo-colonial economic and political dominance.

The pan-Arab visions of a secular political union between Arab states expressed through the Arab League sought to uproot the neo-colonial order and end Western influence. The optimism of independence conceived the possibility of an Arab political bloc regardless of the superpowers' misgivings and preferences for Arab division and impotence. The Arab League attempted to unite distinctive governments through pacts to mediate conflicts and avoid hostilities between member states, agreeing that an attack on one Arab nation would be an attack on all (Treaty of Joint Defence and Economic Cooperation between the States of the Arab League, 1950). The overthrow of the Egyptian monarchy in 1952 was a catalyst for pan-Arabism and revolutionary politics. President Jamal Abdel Nasser was the natural leader due to his popularity in nationalizing the Suez Canal Company; the Tripartite War against Britain, France, and Israel; and his contribution to the development of Third World solidarity. Nasser's political ideology spread through the Arab world and contributed to coup d'états against monarchies and influenced the founding of republics in Tunisia, Iraq, Libya, and

Yemen. Nonetheless, the pan-Arab movement sharply declined in the loss of the Six-Day War and after Nasser's death in 1970.

The failures of pan-Arabism witnessed the rise of Islamic political movements as an alternative. These religious-based movements condemned state control of religious institutions and denounced the negligible implementation of Islamic norms, values, and interpretations into state policies. Islamic movements were popular and reputed to successfully mobilize voters through social programs, charitable campaigns, a keen interest in fighting corruption, and reforming the criminal justice system. Many of the mainstream Islamic movements were willing to accomplish their objectives through political means. However, other radical movement mobilizations utilized violence to seek revolutionary change. The Iranian Revolution and the Afghan War against the Soviet Union amplified Islamic extremism and contributed to political violence in the region. The attacks on 9/11 by the terrorist group Al Qaeda founded by Osama bin Laden put transnational political Islamic movements at the forefront of international attention.

The Bush administration's invasion of Iraq and the U.S. War on Terror reinvigorated pan-Arabism and political Islamic movements. Citizens in the Arab world attentively followed the unfiltered graphic coverage of Iraq's destruction, the treatment of prisoners in Abu Ghraib and Guantanamo Bay, extraordinary rendition, and the international labeling of Arabs as potential terrorists. The carnage of "targeted killings" and drone strikes across the Arab and Muslim world further amplified the region's mistrust and resentment toward the Western coalition and their governments. These policies generated thousands of refugees, killed untold civilians, and, between 2002 and 2014, significantly produced higher prevalence of terrorism than before the advent of the War on Terror (Smith & Zeigler, 2017).

The Arab Spring was an event that reinforced a collective Arab linguistic and political identity but also revealed the extent to which the regimes mobilize criminal justice institutions to sustain power. The anti-government protests against tyrannical rule in Sidi Bouzid, Tunisia, spread to every Arab country through digital technologies and social media. Arab citizens were demoralized by years of human rights violations, police brutality, economic stagnation, unemployment, corruption, and numerous other factors (Kazamias, 2011). The protests eventually deposed rulers in Tunisia, Libya, Egypt, and Yemen with continual uprisings and civil wars. The Arab League was obsolete in solving any issues, and the international community ignored the democratic aspirations of the region's citizens. As time passed, the Arab Spring became the Arab Winter when the monarchies in the region coordinated reactionary counterrevolutions through criminal justice institutions to overcome the imminent threats to their own regimes. The political conditions in Libya, Syria, and Yemen quickly transformed into internationalized civil wars. NATO and the monarchies in the Gulf disintegrated Libya, turning a stable and wealthy nation into a refuge for terrorism, foreign military intervention, and, in certain areas, slavery. Instead of a peaceful solution, the Western and Gulf support for the insurgency expanded terrorist organizations in Syria. Yemen, the poorest country in the Arab world, has experienced a Saudi-led military intervention that has produced the largest humanitarian crisis in modern history (Robinson, 2021).

In the decade following the Arab Spring, optimism was replaced with pessimism. Even Tunisia, the only democratic government in the Arab world, has suffered setbacks, with President Kais Saied dismissing the government, suspending Parliament, and asserting all executive power (Marks et al., 2022). The specter of sectarianism has plagued Iraq, Syria, Lebanon, and Yemen. A solution to the Palestinian/Israeli conflict remains elusive since the normalization of relations in the Abraham Accords between Israel, the United Arab Emirates, Bahrain, Morocco, and Sudan. There is, however, a glimpse of hope in the emergence of anti-regime protests in Sudan, Algeria, Lebanon, and Iraq as an Arab Spring 2.0 (Muasher, 2019).

The fundamental rationale for examining the political nature of the region's regimes is to recognize the arduous conditions of studying criminology in the Arab world (Ouassini & Ouassini, 2020). Academics have numerous challenges in the authoritarian, autocratic, and monarchical regimes that form most contemporary Arab states. Citizens in the Arab world broadly believe in state power and the frequent use of non-democratic solutions to social problems. Alternatively, the criminal justice system is the face of these regimes and the first to execute directives by those in power. The regimes have therefore formulated stringent environments for researchers to capture or employ accurate criminological analysis. In some circumstances, these regimes perceive the denial of access as a mechanism to ensure the semblance of stability. In other cases, the regimes perceive the sharing of data or access to criminological information as potential national security threats against the prevailing power structures and restrict such access to shape crime and justice narratives.

The unsolved murder of Giulio Regeni illustrates the perilous research on sensitive topics in the Arab world (Ragab & al-Marsafawi, 2016). Regeni was an Italian graduate student from Cambridge University studying independent trade unions among food cart vendors in Cairo. His involvement in a politically sensitive topic incurred the attention of the state. In January 2016, Regeni was abducted from Dokki, tortured, and found executed nine days later in Alexandria. Despite evidence of security agents' involvement, the Egyptian government has denied such accusations, and the Italian government continues to search for answers. The Egyptian Ministry of the Interior eventually reported the deaths of four men they claimed were responsible for Regeni's murder. However, these claims faced criticism from the Italian government and the international community. The violent torture and murder of a foreigner conveyed that no one is immune from the regime's wrath in challenging sensitive political issues. Consequently, researchers must constantly seek an equilibrium between their research and the government's security concerns.

The political history that encompasses successive Islamic empires, colonialism, and post-colonial institutional and political bodies and institutions is an important unifying commonality to understand crime and criminal justice in the Arab world. In the discussion on the region's politics, several challenges exist for Arab criminologists, university academics, journalists, civil society organizations, and activists, including the lack of academic freedom, demanding research conditions, and the politicization of research. This is coupled with the unique criminological challenges and questions that exist at the local level through the ongoing impact of sectarianism, authoritarianism, civil wars, mass incarceration, terrorism, and the Arab military–industrial complex.

Cultural Interconnections

The third commonality in developing Arab criminology centers on the ties in the region formulated by an Arab linguistic and cultural identity. Contemporary Arab culture is intricately shaped by multiple characteristics manifested in language, literature, radio, music, television, and cinema (Kraidy, 2008). These cultural mediums gained ground in the 1950s during the popularity of Nasser's pan-Arabism. However, the emergence of Arab satellite programming in the 1990s proliferated Arab news, music, entertainment, and religious channels across the region. During this period, a handful of Arab countries dominated cultural production, framing the narrative on Arab culture and identity (Ayish & Mellor, 2015; Durac, 2015; Khalil & Kraidy, 2017; Ouassini, 2020) by "allowing media content produced in one region . . . [to reflect] its cultural and social norms on the viewers' attitudes and beliefs in other regions" (Kharroub & Weaver, 2019, p. 656). The news coverage from pan-Arab news channels, especially of the Palestinian/Israeli conflict and the U.S. invasion of Iraq, revolutionized broadcast news and how information and identities were featured and consumed by the masses to form modern transnational Arab identities (Bruce & Conlin, 2016). Channels like Al Jazeera provided an Arab perspective on the region's conflicts, challenging Western narratives of the "War on Terror" and Arab government's policies across the region. These technological mediums have sustained and expanded the cultural ties between Arab nations and the so-called

Arab Street, which has continued to expand through the internet and social media as a decentralized form of cultural production.

Arab internet usage has unitized Arabs closer together through social networks, emails, blogs, chats, news and entertainment programs, and transnational movements. Twitter, YouTube, Facebook, and many other social media sites are popular platforms for citizens in the Arab world as a source of entertainment, information, government engagement, and movement mobilizations and are increasingly valuable to netizens bypassing government firewalls as experienced in the Arab Spring. Arab citizens utilized social media platforms to report on the minute-by-minute events, disseminate information, organize protests, and raise international awareness of the on-the ground conditions. The messages, chants, strategies, and other forms of collective action advocating for change corroborate the interactions between activists from varying Arab nations (AlSayyad & Guvenc, 2015). The exchanges signify the importance of Arab media as a cultural medium in promulgating transnational Arab identity as the Arab Spring started in Tunisia and has impacted nearly every Arab nation since. The development of the digital public sphere was a concern for the regimes that conceded the narrative to protestors due to the ineffectiveness of old media, a lack of understanding of the evolution of Arab culture and media, and the traditional strategies of propaganda, intimidation, and repression. Irrespective of the initial successes, many Arab states collectively coordinated a counter-revolution, cracking down on bloggers, journalists, writers, civil society, activists, and any form of online political engagement through new strategies of digital authoritarianism (Dragu & Lupu, 2021).

A critical contribution to Arab criminology will undoubtedly be the development of Arab media, culture, and crime. The porous and conflicting mediated cultural industry, which has encroached upon other criminologies (Laidler et al., 2017), has also taken root in Arab societies (Kraidy, 2008). Ironically, in the Arab world, neoliberalism has further entrenched and actualized a transnational Arab identity, a feat that was previously just an imagined byproduct of pan-Arabism. Thus, the central role that culture plays in the development of Arab criminology cannot be understated. One example wherein Arab cultural criminology can explore is the deep tradition of research in Arab media studies. Most of the research in these outlets has been published through Northern and Arab social scientific journals, with very few studies engaging Arab media from a criminological framework (Bair, 2014; Mahadeen, 2016; Yassni, 2018; Ouassini, 2020). This will entail Arab criminologists to engage the question of how crime is understood, framed, produced, and consumed through these cultural mediums across Arab national contexts. Additionally, this will support "the development of new theoretical and methodological tools that permit the sustained and in-depth engagement with the contemporary media environment" (Greer, 2010, p. 511). Ultimately, allowing Arab criminologists to employ a transdisciplinary framework that considers Northern, Southern, and decolonial perspectives to fashion an Arab cultural criminology captures the impact of culture, media, and crime in the collective Arab imagined community, while also recognizing local communities and their agency over cultural production in the face of globalization (Mellor et al., 2011; Kim & Lim, 2019; Hurley, 2021).

The cultural ties underlying the Arab nations and peoples provide Arab criminology new and dynamic ways of engaging crime in the Arab world (Fraser et al., 2017, p. 2). This includes comparative and cross-national perspectives on criminalization of culture and cultural practices (Fraser et al., 2017, p. 2), for example, the recent efforts in Sudan to decriminalize the practice of FGM (Tiwary, 2020), or the case of Weld El 15, a Tunisian hip-hop artist who was arrested and jailed in 2013 for his song "Police Are Dogs." The government claimed his music incited hatred, violence, and disorder against the police and magistrates and sought to criminalize his speech (Nielson, 2013). Cultural resistance and contestations in the Arab world have produced a slew of laws that have criminalized and decriminalized cultural practices. In Egypt, the passing of the broad-based cybersecurity laws was used to arrest and prosecute a number of TikTok stars for posting lewd videos (Khalil, 2020). In recent years, the U.A.E. has decriminalized suicide and alcohol with the intention to uphold major reforms with regard to personal status laws (Qiblawi, 2020). These changes reflect the general contestations from the business community, tourists, expatriates, and global civil society.

Arab collective memory is another cultural component important for the development of an Arab criminology (Fraser et al., 2017, p. 2) "in shaping public attitudes towards crime and justice, and especially how diverse pasts are mobilized by different social groups" (Churchill, 2017, p. 8). The experiences of vulgar violence and conflict in the Arab world has produced new contestations over truth narratives and representation. Haugbolle and Hastrup (2008) explain that the cultural memories of the Abu Ghraib correctional facility became the symbolic frame from which Iraqis and Arabs mobilize when discussing the American invasion and occupation of Iraq. Ultimately, the way Arab nations and minority communities engage these cultural memories in connection with their experiences with violence, state repression, genocide, ethnic cleansing, slavery, civil war, and terrorism will shape how contemporary Arab states overcome, reform, and heal their societies.

Conclusion

This chapter argues that the historical, political, and cultural commonalities between Arab states necessitate the establishment of an Arab criminology. This would require Arab criminologists to correlate history to the current systems to understand the interactions and hybridization of the criminal justice, legal, and political systems at the local and regional levels. The pre-colonial, colonial, and post-colonial periods need further exploration as social scientists become more attentive to Islamic, colonial, and post-colonial legacies and influences (Ciocchini & Greener, 2021). The study of Arab criminology also requires an awareness of the current political characteristics of the region's regimes. The ideology of Arab nationalism and the formation of the Arab League have contributed to the enduring politics in the region. Regrettably, the authoritarian nature of most regimes in the region will entail demanding conditions when conducting criminological research. Finally, the contemporary developments in Arab culture and media industry are increasingly shaping crime and criminal justice systems, collective memory, and cultural processes that include resistance, contestations, and interconnections.

References

Albirini, A. (2020). Language-identity dynamics in post-Arab Spring era: The case of Jordan. In R. Bassiouney & K. Walters (Eds.), *The Routledge handbook of Arabic and identity* (pp. 176–193). Routledge.

Alistair, H. (2012). *A savage war of peace Algeria 1954–1962*. Pan Macmillan.

Alleg, H. (2006). *The question*. University of Nebraska Press.

AlSayyad, N., & Guvenc, M. (2015). Virtual uprisings: On the interaction of new social media, traditional media coverage and urban space during the 'Arab Spring'. *Urban Studies*, *52*(11), 2018–2034.

Ayish, M., & Mellor, N. (2015). *Reporting in the MENA region: Cyber engagement and pan-Arab social media*. Rowman & Littlefield.

Bair, M. (2014, September 23). Navigating the Ethics of Citizen Video: The Case of a Sexual Assault in Egypt. *Arab Media & Society*, 19, 1–7. https://www.arabmediasociety.com/navigating-the-ethics-of-citizen-video-the-case-of-a-sexual-assault-in-egypt/

Bitar, S. I. (2011). Language, identity, and Arab nationalism: Case study of Palestine. *Journal of Middle Eastern and Islamic Studies (in Asia)*, *5*(4), 48–64.

Blankinship, K. Y. (1994). *The end of the Jihad state: The reign of Hisham Ibn 'Abd al-Malik and the collapse of the Umayyads*. SUNY Press.

Bruce, M. D., & Conlin, L. (2016). Images of conflict and explicit violence on Arab TV: A visual content analysis of five pan-Arab news networks. *Athens Journal of Mass Media and Communications*, *2*(3), 151–168. https://doi.org/10.30958/ajmmc.2.3.1

Choueiri, Y. (2000). *Arab nationalism: A history: Nation and state in the Arab world*. Blackwell Publishers.

Churchill, D. (2017). Towards historical criminology. *Crime, History & Societies*, *21*(2), 379–386. https://doi.org/10.4000/chs.2056

Ciocchini, P., & Greener, J. (2021). Mapping the pains of neo-colonialism: A critical elaboration of southern criminology. *The British Journal of Criminology*, *61*(6), 1612–1629.

Debre, M. J. (2021). Legitimation, regime survival, and shifting alliances in the Arab League: Explaining sanction politics during the Arab Spring. *International Political Science Review*, *42*(4), 516–530.

Dragu, T., & Lupu, Y. (2021). Digital authoritarianism and the future of human rights. *International Organization*, *75*(4), 991–1017.

Durac, V. (2015). Social movements, protest movements and cross-ideological coalitions–the Arab uprisings re-appraised. *Democratization*, *22*(2), 239–258.

El-Azhari, T. (2019). *Queens, eunuchs and concubines in Islamic history, 661–1257*. Edinburgh University Press.

Elgawly, M. M. (2017). Realism and Arab nationalism: An uneasy partnership. *Inquiries Journal*, *9*(12).

Fraser, A., Lee, M., & Tang, D. (2017). Crime, media, culture: Asia-style. *Crime, Media, Culture: An International Journal*, *13*(2), 131–134. https://doi.org/10.1177/1741659017718975

Greer, C. (2010). 'News Media Criminology.' In E. McLaughlin & T. Newburn, (Eds). *The Sage Handbook of Criminological Theory*. London: Sage (pp. 490–513).

Halliday, F. (2013). Nationalism in the Arab world since 1945. In J. Breuilly (Ed.), *The Oxford handbook of the history of nationalism* (pp. 435–452). Oxford University Press.

Harik, I. (2006). The origins of the Arab state system. In G. Salame (Ed.), *The foundations of the Arab state* (pp. 19–46). Routledge.

Haugbolle, S., & Hastrup, A. (2008). Introduction: Outlines of a new politics of memory in the Middle East. *Mediterranean Politics*, *13*(2), 133–149. https://doi.org/10.1080/13629390802127497

Helms, C. M. (1990). *Arabism and Islam: Stateless nations and nationless*. Diane Publishing Company.

Hurley, Z. (2021). # reimagining Arab women's social media empowerment and the postdigital condition. *Social Media+ Society*, *7*(2).

Kazamias, A. (2011). The 'anger revolutions' in the Middle East: An answer to decades of failed reform. *Journal of Balkan and Near Eastern Studies*, *13*(2), 143–156.

Khalil, J. (2020, September 18). Social media censorship in Egypt targets women on TikTok. *The World*. https://theworld.org/stories/2020-09-18/social-media-censorship-egypt-targets-women-tiktok

Khalil, J. F., & Kraidy, M. M. (2017). *Arab television industries*. Bloomsbury Publishing.

Kharroub, T., & Weaver, A. J. (2019). Selective exposure and perceived identification with characters in transnational Arabic television. *International Journal of Communication*, *13*, 21.

Kiernan, B. (2008). *Blood and soil: A world history of genocide and extermination from Sparta to Darfur*. Yale University Press.
Kim, H. H. S., & Lim, C. (2019). From virtual space to public space: The role of online political activism in protest participation during the Arab Spring. *International Journal of Comparative Sociology*, *60*(6), 409–434.
Kraidy, M. M. (2008). Youth, media and culture in the Arab world. In K. Drotner & S. Livingstone (Eds.), *International handbook of children, media and culture* (pp. 330–344). Sage. http://repository.upenn.edu/asc_papers/307
Kramer, M. (1993). Arab nationalism: Mistaken identity. *Daedalus*, 171–206.
Laidler, K. J., Lee, M., & Wong, G. P. (2017). Doing criminology on media and crime in Asia. *Crime, Media, Culture*, *13*(2), 135–151. https://doi.org/10.1177/1741659017710296
Lohlker, R. (2016). Jamāʻa vs. Mulk: Community-Centred and Ruler-Centred Visions of the Islamic Community. In E. Hovden, C. Lutter, & W. Pohl (Eds.), *Meanings of community across Medieval Eurasia* (pp. 78–96). Brill.
Mabry, T. J. (2015). *Nationalism, language, and Muslim exceptionalism*. University of Pennsylvania Press.
Mahadeen, E. (2016). 'The martyr of dawn': Femicide in Jordanian media. *Crime, Media, Culture: An International Journal*, *13*(1), 41–54. https://doi.org/10.1177/1741659016643120
Mahoney, D. (2016). The political construction of a tribal genealogy from early medieval south Arabia. In E. Hovden, C. Lutter, & W. Pohl (Eds.), *Meanings of community across Medieval Eurasia* (pp. 163–182). Brill.
Mamdani, M. (2018). *Citizen and subject*. Princeton University Press.
Marks, M., Masmoudi, R. A., Bandow, D., & Akyol, M. (2022, October 25). Tunisia's authoritarian turn. *Cato Institute*. https://policycommons.net/artifacts/2610944/tunisias-authoritarian-turn/3633505/
Masters, B. (2013). *The Arabs of the Ottoman empire, 1516–1918: A social and cultural history*. Cambridge University Press.
Masters, J., & Sergie, M. A. (2020, February 19). The Arab league. *Council on Foreign Relations*. www.cfr.org/backgrounder/arab-league
Mellor, N., Rinnawi, K., Dajani, N., & Ayish, M. I. (2011). *Arab media: Globalization and emerging media industries* (Vol. 1). Polity.
Muasher, M. (2019, October 30). Is this the Arab Spring 2.0? Beirut. *Carnegie Endowment for International Peace*. https://carnegieendowment.org/2019/10/30/is-this-arab-spring-2.0-pub–80220
Nielson, E. (2013, July 1). Arab rappers are landing in jail for lyrics – kind of like American rappers. *The Atlantic*. www.theatlantic.com/entertainment/archive/2013/07/arab-rappers-are-landing-in-jail-for-lyrics-kind-of-like-american-rappers/277448/
Ouassini, A. (2020). The Ummah racial project: Arab satellite television, Islamic movements, and the construction of Spanish Moroccan identity. *Ethnic and Racial Studies*, *43*(4), 751–767.
Ouassini, N., & Ouassini, A. (2020). Criminology in the Arab world: Misconceptions, nuances and future prospects. *The British Journal of Criminology*, *60*(3), 519–536.

Pact of the League of Arab States. (1945, March 22). Yale Lillian Goldman law library. *The Avalon Project*. https://avalon.law.yale.edu/20th_century/arableag.asp

Qiblawi, T. (2020, November 10). The UAE takes steps towards modernization by decriminalizing alcohol and suicide. *CNN*. https://edition.cnn.com/2020/11/09/middleeeast/uae-decriminalize-alcohol-suicide-intl/index.html

Ragab, A., & al-Marsafawi, M. (2016, July 3). Giulio Regeni: Scattered facts. *Jadaliyya*. www.jadaliyya.com/pages/index/24019/giulio-regeni_scattered-facts

Renima A., Tiliouine H., & Estes R.J. (2016). The Islamic golden age: A story of the triumph of the Islamic civilization. In H. Tiliouine & R. Estes (Eds.), *The state of social progress of Islamic societies. International handbooks of quality-of-life* (pp. 25–52). Springer.

Robinson, K. (2021). How severe is Yemen's humanitarian crisis? *Council on Foreign Relations*. www.jstor.org/stable/pdf/resrep29956.pdf

Smith, M., & Zeigler, S. M. (2017). Terrorism before and after 9/11 – a more dangerous world? *Research & Politics*, *4*(4). https://doi.org/10.1177%2F2053168017739757

Sulaiman, S. J. (2007). The Arab identity. *Al-Hewar, the Arab American Dialogue*. www.alhewar.net/Basket/Sadek_Sulaiman-ARAB_IDENTITY

Suleiman, Y. (Ed.). (1994). *Arabic sociolinguistics: Issues and perspectives*. Curzon Press.

Suleiman, Y. (2004). *A war of words: Language and conflict in the Middle East*. Cambridge University Press.

Tibi, B. (1997). *Arab nationalism: A critical enquiry*.: Macmillan.

Tiwary, A. (2020, June 9). The criminalization of female genital mutilation in Sudan. *JURIST – Commentary – Legal News & Commentary*. www.jurist.org/commentary/2020/06/akshita-tiwary-female-genital-mutilation/

Webb, W. P. (2016). *Imagining the Arabs: Arab identity and the rise of Islam*. Edinburgh University Press. https://doi.org/10.1177/1741659016643120

Yassni, Y. (2018, October 6). Youth in Morocco: Rebels without a cause? Youth violence, social media, and the discontents of Moroccan consumer society. *Arab Media & Society*. www.arabmediasociety.com/youth-in-morocco-rebels-without-a-cause-youth-violence-social-media-and-the-discontents-of-moroccan-consumer-society/

4 Arab Criminology at the Intersection of Race and Gender

Introduction: Race and Crime in the Arab World

The study of race as a process of human categorization and organization is relatively new in the Arab world (Aidi et al., 2020), especially when linked with the study of crime and criminality (Ouassini & Ouassini, 2020). The primary reasons why this has been the case include the lingering Orientalist theoretical frameworks that conceptualize the Arab world as a homogenous entity primarily racialized through an Islamic religious lens (Said, 1978; Aziz, 2021). However, a more nuanced understanding of the Arab world would reveal that race is an overlooked topic of research that needs to be explored and developed as it can profoundly impact how criminologists understand crime and criminal justice systems (Carrington et al., 2018; Ouassini & Ouassini, 2020; Aidi et al., 2021). Indeed, this is important as the centrality of racial theoretical orientations in Northern criminal justice systems reveals that race and racial projects "remain at the core of criminological knowledge production" (León, 2021, p. 388). In fact, as Scott et al. state, "[W]ithout race, modern criminology is impossible" (2018, p. 158; Lafree & Russell, 1993; Bowling & Phillips, 2003). The dearth of research in Northern criminological scholarship on race and crime reveals its centrality to the discipline (Lafree & Russell, 1993; Brown & Barganier, 2018; Sampson et al., 2018). It also lends credence to why it is critical in the development of Arab criminology to understand how race may inform its evolution and development (Ouassini & Ouassini, 2020). Still, across the Arab and Northern social sciences, minimal studies explore race as a variable of exploration in the Arab world (Aidi et al., 2021); thus, it is essential to understand how it can shape the potential growth of Arab criminology (Ouassini & Ouassini, 2020).

The recent shift toward a global perspective on race and racialization as a framework of study in the Arab world has "opened the door for important comparative insights and new understandings about the mechanisms and

DOI: 10.4324/9781003169789-4

legacies of marginalization and exclusion across regions" (Aidi et al., 2021, p. 3). The importance of understanding racialization in the Arab world will provide context to the process wherein racial meaning is applied "to a previously racially unclassified relationship, social practice, or group" (Omi & Winant, 1986, p. 111). For example, the central role that racial ideologies played in the forging and expansion of the Islamic empires from Arabia in the 7th century still reverberates in the legal and cultural frameworks throughout the Middle East and North Africa today (Lewis, 1990; King, 2019). Until recently, Northern and Arab social scientific research has emphasized religious variables to explain social, historical, and political phenomena in the Arab world (Lewis, 1976; Lockman, 2004; Kalmar, 2013), hence reflecting the deeply embedded colonial and post-colonial Orientalist tradition that historically racialized the Arabs through a Muslim-first identity framework (Samiei, 2010; Abulhab, 2011). Untangling these Northern intellectual traditions from the Arab world and looking at these processes as they are on the ground will reveal that race is an important framework shaping contemporary Arab societies and thus has a tremendous impact on the development of Arab criminology (Aidi et al., 2021; Ozcelik, 2021).

As a result of these developments, the democratization of knowledge (Carrington et al., 2016) will be necessary between the criminologies to engage and exchange theoretical frameworks to understand the intricacies of race in Arab criminological phenomenon. Notwithstanding, there is apprehension that Arab scholars and scholars of the Arab world may impose Northern discourse and language on race and "racializations" (Ozcelik, 2021). However, the ongoing development of social sciences and the humanities in the Arab world will ultimately necessitate new and dynamic concepts that can allow researchers to contend with, engage in, formulate, and act upon the ways that race and racialization processes significantly shape criminological areas of interest. These potentially include racialized processes embedded in law and legal systems, punishment, crime, criminal justice administration, victimization, and policing.

Thus, understanding race and crime outside the conceptual toolbox that race studies in the North have primarily established will allow Arab criminologists to move beyond a "narrow empirical base" that scholars of race often depend on (Telles, 2014, p. 2). While in the past few decades, the body of Northern criminological literature on race and crime has been quite "durable" in its growth and expansion (Scott et al., 2018, p. 156), comparable evidence from the Arab world has been non-existent in both the Arabic and English languages (Ouassini & Ouassini, 2020). It is of utmost importance that Arab criminology considers race as "highly variable, both culturally and historically" (Scott et al., 2018, p. 156), as all empires in the

Arab world have employed racial projects to structure economic, social, and political arrangements in their societies (Lewis, 1990; King, 2019). Specifically, this will necessitate that research on race, racialization, and crime move beyond the black–white racial binary dominant in Northern criminology (Perea, 1997).

In fact, even Arab conceptualizations of whiteness have appeared in Islamic and Arab literature before the onset of European colonialism, revealing the existence of non-European historicity of whiteness as one of many strands of racial ideological formations present in the Arab world (Hopper, 2015; Freamon, 2021; Brown, 2019). Nevertheless, moving beyond the static categories established about the Arab world from Northern social science traditions will allow Arab criminologists to explore the fluidity of racial categories and capture the diversity and heterogenous reality of race as a categorical framework in relation to crime. Namely, this will dehomogenize (Phillips & Bowling, 2003) the imagined Arab racial category to expand its discursive possibilities to inform the researcher of their multiple expressions.

Race and Arab Criminology

If racial projects have always been a part of the Arab world, why has it been ignored, and more importantly, what historical and contemporary role has it played in Arab criminal justice systems? In the contemporary Arab world, racializing practices have emanated from the (1) fact of conquest, which initially divided the Arabs from the non-Arabs (Brown, 2019); (2) European colonization (Silverstein, 2002); (3) the Arab slave trade (Lewis, 1990; King, 2019); (4) the rise of Arabism, which has reached beyond the "confines of the of the MENA region" (Aidi et al., 2021); and (5) global white supremacy (Christian, 2019). These factors have historically centralized the role of race in the fabric of Arab society and have continually played a prominent role in influencing and shaping criminal justice institutions (Ouassini & Ouassini, 2020). Thus, in moving beyond the privileged Northern epistemologies of race and racialization and understanding the limited work completed on race and crime in the Arab world (Ozcelik, 2021; Aidi et al., 2021), it is essential to work through and build on a transdisciplinary framework inclusive of Northern and Southern social science disciplines particularly sociology, anthropology, political science, and history (Bleakley & Kehoe, 2021).

A transdisciplinary framework will allow researchers in both the North and South to approach the study of race and crime in the Arab world through multiple prisms to build theory, including the exploration of the ongoing race research on anti-refugee violence in Lebanon ("Lebanon: Rising

Violence Targets Syrian Refugees," 2020) and the centrality of genealogy in structuring society, mobility, and racial minority access to justice in the U.A.E. (Lori & Kuzmova, 2021). It would also expound on culturally based interpretations of race that are directly influenced by the hybridization of global white supremacy and traditional Arab racial ideologies, including anti-black racism and slavery (Mafu, 2019), and vulgar violence and ethnic cleansing in Darfur through racial projects emanating from a collective imagined membership to an Arab tribe and language (Shrkey, H.J. 2008). For example, Mazrui (1969) explains that in the Arab tradition, the primacy of the Arabic language is a critical component of Arabness in the Sudan, reflecting the same linguistic definition employed by the Arab League, superimposing Arab identity on large populations in the Middle East and Africa, while not considering the geographic, tribal, and racial variations (Ouassini & Ouassini, 2020).

The importance of integrating race and racialization frameworks in Arab criminology will expound on a critical sociodemographic variable shaping crime, criminality, and criminal justice administration. It will ultimately demonstrate the "powerful and longstanding dialectical relationship between race and crime" (Phillips et al., 2020, p. 428) in the Arab world. While race and crime are deeply researched in Northern criminology, it is imperative that Arab criminology not turn its gaze away from race in developing Arab criminological scholarship. Understanding Arab racial projects will aid the subdiscipline in moving away from Northern "criminology's suppressions, contradictions and lacunae regarding race and racism" (Phillips et al., 2020, p. 429) and localize it within the Arab world. Arab criminologists can accomplish this by approaching race as a key variable in analysis and theoretical construction while also considering whether "such groups can be considered discrete, measurable, and scientifically meaningful" (Scott et al., 2018, p. 159). This is especially important as there is a need to advance and expand the discipline beyond the black-and-white binary (Hesse, 2014, p. 143) that essentially reduces race and racial identity to phenotype or a group's physical features (Phillips, 2020, p. 436), which does not capture or represent the lived realities of racial minorities/majorities in the Arab world. As Mazrui (1969, p. 167) has observed, "[T]he Arabs as a race . . . defy straight pigmentational classifications. They vary in color from white Arabs of Syria and Lebanon, brown Arabs of Hadramaut, to the black Arabs of the Sudan." One way we can understand this is by peering into specific developments in the Arab world to understand how racial dynamics may inform the development of Arab criminology.

In Janmyr's seminal work (2016), she reveals how the construction of contemporary Egyptian national identity has led to a systematic dismissal and erasure of the Nubian Black population from the Egyptian political, social, and economic life. The ramification of these racialized policies has led to bouts of brutal police violence against the Egyptian Nubian community. In 2017, Egyptian police arrested 24 Nubian activists, wherein Gamal Sorour, one of the leading activists, died in prison due to medical negligence (Holmes, 2018). The subsequent protest and mobilizations by the Nubian community increased police brutality, judicial harassment, and ongoing hate crimes. In Yemen, colorism and the embedded caste systems have created a culture wherein Black *Muhamasheen* Yemenis are racialized and labeled as criminals, misfits, and violent offenders. The state's targeted discrimination of the *Muhamasheen* is primarily employed through state and criminal justice actors to actively deny basic services to the community (Al-Warraq, 2019). In North African states, including Morocco, Algeria, and Mauritania, French colonization policies have historically divided the Berber and Arab populations along racial and ethnic lines, leading to contemporary ethnic and racial divisions that have often spurred communal violence and tension between the communities and the criminal justice system (Silverstein, 2002). In Mauritania, research on the Haratin is producing new approaches of conceptualizing racial identity as this work seeks to deconstruct the racialized slave-based system imposed in Mauritania due to cultural Arabism in the region. In fact, nearly 340,000–680,000 Mauritanians are enslaved out of a population of 3.4 million (Sutter, 2012, p. 38). Across the Sahara, the re-emergence of slavery in post-Qaddafi Libya has been influenced by the steep racial and political conflict that has continually shaped Libyan society. In 2017, the international community was outraged at the emergence of slave markets wherein sub-Saharan African migrants heading north to Italy were captured, enslaved, and sold (Mafu, 2019).

For this reason, emphasizing the role of race, racial projects, and racialization processes in shaping criminal justice actors, institutions, and practices may also facilitate a paradigm shift in Arab academia to take the study of race seriously. Namely, how critical it is in the construction of Arab identity. This can allow Arab criminologists and social scientists to re-evaluate and expand on topics and studies often approached through Northern Orientalist and political science theoretical frameworks. For example, reading race and racialization into the study of state-led violence campaigns can produce alternative narratives that can provide new insights and theories to understand and address the phenomena. This is evidenced, for example, through Saddam Hussein's genocidal policies and actions toward the racialized Shi'a and Kurdish communities; Sudan's Omar Al Bashir's support of the Arab Janjaweed violent campaigns against the Darfurians; and the racial dynamics underlying the Israeli occupation of the West Bank and Gaza Strip. Just as important, this violence is underscored through racial projects embedded in the criminal justice systems that sustain the violent apparatus through mass incarceration, police brutality, and sham court processes, which allows for the implementation of this state-led violence.

In the Arab Gulf, the *Kafala* system is a practice in which individual citizens have complete control over the employment of immigrants including forced laborers and maids (Strobl, 2009; Al Shehabi, 2019; Fernandez, 2021). This system demands the employed to give up their passports, sign contracts that they are not able to comprehend because of the language barriers, and are actively criminalized for absconding ("Qatar: Significant Labor and Kafala Reforms," 2020). All of this has caused widespread domestic violence and exploitation of these racial and ethnic migrant communities who have no legal recourse and face a criminal justice system that sides with the nationals in arbitration regarding contracts, payments, and accusations of violence. Moreover, these immigrants are often considerably overrepresented in the criminal justice system, leading to what many scholars argue as systemic "legalized slavery" (Zaraket, 2020). In Bahrain, the minority ruling Sunni elite continue a British colonial practice of hiring police and other criminal justice actors from Sunni Pakistani and Arab communities to maintain control of the majority Bahraini Shi'a population (Strobl, 2011). By and large, this allows the state to reinforce the minority Sunni Arab regime's dominance and racializes Shi'a Arabs as the Other (Hasso, 2016). The consequence of such a policy has sustained decades of police brutality and indiscriminate police violence against Shi'a communities.

Finally, the impact of global racial scapes emanating from the United States has trickled into Arab societies. Arab minorities in Israel and the Palestinian citizens of the West Bank and Gaza Strip have co-opted and embraced the Black Lives Matter frame as they bridge grievances with African American communities across the transnational chain, in order to bring light to their daily struggles with police brutality, stop and frisk, checkpoints, discriminatory practices in the justice system, and vulgar state violence (Sato & Moser, 2022). For example, the discourse on the occupation of the Gaza Strip, which is about 141 square miles, is described as an open-air prison in which all Gazan bodies are watched, controlled, punished, and denigrated by the Israeli political and military machine ("Gaza: Israel's 'Open-Air Prison' at 15," 2022).

The Future of Race and Crime in the Arab World

The existing gaps in the research in the study of race in the Arab social sciences are compounded by the nearly non-existent literature on race and crime and criminal justice systems. The task of Arab criminology in integrating theories of race into the disciplinary contours of Arab criminology will provide critical attention to the lived realities in the Arab world.

Moreover, it will address how race and racial projects are constructed and embedded in criminal justice processes and administration. More importantly, the operationalization of race will differ from the structural approaches that have dominated the Northern tradition and will reflect, as discussed, the differing historical-socio-political contexts of the Arab world (Scott et al., 2018, 160). Ultimately, this will bring attention to and accommodate an analysis for the discussion around the historical amnesia surrounding slavery in the Arab world, racial and ethnic disparities in corrections, policing, administration of justice, impact of Arab racialization frameworks on criminalization, and endemic state violence. Furthermore, additional areas to be explored include how racial biologism through tribal and genealogical ties impacts legal and social frameworks, overrepresentation of minority communities in the criminal justice system, racialized characterizations of criminality, institutional racism, and minority community marginalization (Scott et al., 2018, p. 159). Ultimately, the subdiscipline of Arab criminology must emphasize the importance of integrating localized racial projects in generating new criminological and social-scientific research.

Gender and Crime in the Arab World

There have been extensive developments in academic research on gender in the Arab world (Kulwicki, 2002; Abu Odeh, 2010; Abadeer, 2015; Yassine-Hamdan, 2020), specifically on gender and politics (Pepicelli, 2017), social movements (Ohansson-Nogués, 2013; Makdisi, 2014), feminist inquiry (Al-Ghanim, 2013, Zaatari, 2014), religion (Charrad, 2011, Lomazzi, 2020), gendered violence (Lafta et al., 2009; Ali et al., 2014; Elghossain et al., 2019), and the family (Haj-Yahia & Clark, 2013; Clark et al., 2009; Al-Badayneh, 2012, Alsaleh, 2015). However, very little has been published on the relationship between gender and crime and criminal justice systems from within the discipline of criminology in the Arab world (Ouassini & Ouassini, 2020). The minimal research has been framed through a Northern framework, often focusing on the politics of domestic violence (Ennaji & Sadiqi, 2011; Shiraz, 2016; Douki et al., 2021), honor killings (Kulwicki, 2002; Abu Odeh, 2010), rape (Tonnessen, 2014; Haddad, 2017; Ouassini, 2019), sexual harassment (Chafai, 2017; Tillous & Lachenal, 2021), and terrorism and conflict (Holt & Jawad, 2013), from within a "gaze of domestic issues in criminal justice" (Carrington et al., 2016). Consequently, this literature on gender and crime in the Arab world has only reproduced "concepts embedded in North thinking" (Carrington et al., 2016), traditional Islamic theological and jurisprudential frameworks (Kamali, 2015), and emerging Northern feminists' theoretical orientations (Arfaoui, 2016).

The integration of gender as a sociodemographic variable in Arab criminological research would necessitate engaging with Arab and Islamic feminist epistemologies (Arfaoui, 2016), localized experiences with patriarchy, and engaging gender within lived contexts. This is important as it will impact Arab criminological knowledge production and challenge Northern and Southern claims on gender in the Arab world (Ennaji & Sadiqi, 2011). Ultimately, this will entail deconstructing existing ideological frameworks that are remnants of Northern theoretical perspectives that often focus on the role of Islamic law and culture as primary agents shaping gendered processes. Arab criminology must integrate the racial, ethnic, class, and religious diversity present in Arab women's intersectional identities and experiences. This will necessitate new theoretical and methodological considerations from within the Arab world as opposed to reproducing "totalizing concepts that travel from North to South and West to East, silencing difference and emphasizing sameness" (Barberet & Carrington, 2018, p. 823). In turn, Arab criminologists and scholars of the Arab world will "widen its research agendas to include the distinctively different gendered patterns of crime and violence" in the Arab world (Carrington, et al., 2016, p. 2), contributing to a grounded approach toward understanding gender and crime in the Arab world and not perpetuate the Northern gaze or superimpose orientalist imaginations about Arab women that are neither theoretically sound nor reflect their lives.

Gender-Based Violence in the Arab World

Like the Northern criminological tradition, the research on gender-based violence (GBV) published in the Arab world has focused on intimate partner violence and criminal justice reform (Lafta et al., 2009; Ennaji & Sadiqi, 2011; Elghossain, et al., 2019). The focus on GBV and the recent attempts to pursue legal reforms by state and civil society have been emerging themes of the literature on women and crime in the Arab World (Ouassini, 2021). While the current research is primarily based out of the Global North by scholars of the Arab world and NGO documentation, there have been extensive developments among Indigenous Arab scholars researching Arab women and crime. While gender and crime research that emanates from the Arab world has made a dent in the development of Arab criminology, it has sustained the logic and epistemological frameworks of Northern social sciences. Outside of the development of Islamic feminist inquiry and Islamic scholarship, there has not been a sustained effort at generating theory from the ground (Connell, 2006, p. 215). One of the first journals to address the question of gender and crime in the Arab world is the journal *Al-Raida*, published by the Arab Institute for Women at the Lebanese American University in Lebanon. It has produced several of the earliest studies by Arab Women exploring the question of gender and crime in the Arab world. One of the journal's seminal articles describing the state of gender and crime in the Arab world argues that three main issues shape the minimal research on female offenders:

> [T]he Arab World is mainly constituted of third-world countries where the state is, or should be, primarily preoccupied with providing its people their basic rights (food, shelter, clothing, health, etc.). This fact prevents the state from allocating enough time and resources to solve issues such as female criminality. Second, the fact that the rate and gravity of male criminality are usually higher than female criminality; therefore, time and effort allocated to research male criminality issues are given priority. The third reason is the underestimation of the competence and proficiency of women in the Arab World. This misled presumption also inversely assumes that since women are not as physically capable as men then their capacity to commit crimes is, therefore, lower.
>
> (Mohanna, 2006, p. 50)

Thus, there is a need to consider the socio-political sphere along with context-specific variables shaping gender and crime, including class, family, religion, tribe, and culture. This provides a starting place for scholars to begin engaging with and understanding gender and crime in Arab national contexts. Approaching these distinctions from outside the Northern gaze will reveal the agency Arab women have and the variations in their experiences and engagement with crime from within a collective and individual framework. Moreover, this informs the gender-based challenges that exist for women working in the criminal justice system in the Arab world as more research needs to explore the lack of women in criminal justice institutions.

Arab Women as Victims and Offenders of Crime

While minimal public data exists in the Arab world capturing gender-based violence and the victimization of women, there has been excellent research produced, mainly by nonprofits, transnational NGOs, and regional and international think tanks (ESCWA-UN, 2017; UN Women, 2013). Understanding Arab women's experiences of victimization, both violent and psychological trauma, is essential as minimal resources and attention are utilized to address the needs of victims across Arab national contexts (Strobl, 2006). Moreover, it is crucial to consider the various forms of GBV that are specific to the Arab world as a result of conflict or cultural norms, including honor killings (Kulczycki & Windle, 2011), sexual slavery (El-Masri, 2021), FGM (Refaat et al., 2001), forced marriages and separations (Tapper & Tapper, 1992), immigration and trafficking (Mahdavi & Sargent, 2011), and violence imposed in the context of war (Carrington, et al., 2016).

Understanding these variables in their culturally specific context is critical to understanding gender and crime in the Arab world. According to a 2010 survey, 47% of women have experienced domestic violence in Tunisia ("Tunisia: Landmark Step to Shield Women From Violence," 2022), while in Egypt, "more than 70 percent of men and women said they believe that wives should tolerate violence to keep the family together" ("Egypt," 2017, p. 15). In Jordan, where femicide via honor killings is normalized in some rural communities, it was found that not only are tribal cultural beliefs and practices justifying these killings, but they are also often sustained via the media (Mahadeen, 2017). In Morocco, a national survey found that only 3 out of 100 women survivors of sexual assault reported incidents to police institutions (UNSDG, 2021) for fear of the cultural stigmatization attached to sexual assault in Moroccan society. While these statistics are not specific to only the Arab world, the cultural frameworks governing these practices must be explored and uncovered to underscore their patriarchal and often colonial roots to produce new ways that Arab criminologists can capture these processes as they produce new research and policy frameworks.

As offenders, Arab women are more likely to engage in similar crimes as women in Northern and Southern nations, including prostitution, drug trafficking, and forgery as well as in violent acts, often within the proscribed criminal roles that women may hold in Arab societies. These include enslavers, physical abuse of servants, terrorism, murder, and child abuse. For example, in Bahrain, Strobl (2006, p. 19) found that most of the female population incarcerated are of South Asian descent, often working as domestic servants who attempt to get "away from sponsors due to physical and sexual abuse, being overworked and their salaries being withheld." Often in contexts like Bahrain, the emphasis is on South Asian minority women "breaking the law" as opposed to being victims of the aforementioned Kafala system.

Alternatively, Mohanna (2006) describes crimes wherein Arab women participate that violate proscribed roles and lead to punishments within the criminal justice system and the communities in which they belong. She states, "[L]ong years of civil wars, world wars, and historical wars in the Arab region let women witness continuous horrible atrocities and unjust acts where the value of the human being deteriorated. Those acts against humanity did influence women to take revenge and ensure their self-defense through crimes; especially in order to protect their children" (52). These violent acts are performed by Arab women who are a byproduct of the violence they now employ. In Iraq, thousands of Yazidi women were captured, enslaved, and sold as sex slaves or forced into marriages under the Islamic State (ISIS). Wives of the Islamic state soldiers, who in many cases themselves had been forced into marriages or trafficked into Syria and Iraq, would groom and aid in the enslavement of the Yazidi girls and women (El-Masri, 2021). Consequently, this is important as the Northern literature has established that the actions of these women and how the criminal justice system labels and processes these actions are often from an offender's perspective, ignoring the ongoing victimization of these women.

Gender and Policing

One area of exploration that will be key to understanding the role of gender in the development of Arab criminology is policing. The literature on gender and policing in the Arab world is few and far behind; however, it is probably one of the most developed areas, notwithstanding that policing in the Global North and South has been historically and contemporarily gendered. There has been a concerted effort across the Arab world to be more inclusive of women in policing institutions. The objectives are to address gender disparities, especially as they relate to gender-based violence and the rise of female offenders, and to create an atmosphere for women to communicate and share their experiences without violating their honor or experiencing shame. These reforms are coupled with recent phenomena across the Arab world wherein policing institutions targeted and shamed women held in their custody. Under Egyptian president Sisi's regime, policing institutions have been complicit in harassing and sexually assaulting women, not addressing their issues and complaints seriously, conducting virginity exams to shame and potentially prosecute women for adultery, and failing to recognize the rampant scourge of sexual harassment throughout major Egyptian cities (UN Women, 2013).

In response to the domestic and international outrage, the Egyptian government deployed female police officers in and around cinemas and other high-traffic areas during festivals, celebrations, and the Eid El-Fitr to curb sexual harassment against women (Hussein, 2018). This is especially important in contexts like Egypt and other Arab nations, where victims of sexual assault must report the incident in front of multiple people (primarily males), which often deters women from reporting because of the shame and the cultural attitudes that may exist regarding sexual assault regardless of one's identity, age, or religious affiliation (Khattab & Myrttinen 2014). The researchers (2014, p. 6) found that

> female officers are thus perceived as being more approachable than their male counterparts, and their presence would also alleviate sociocultural concerns of women entering heavily male-dominated spaces. Having more female officers could encourage more women, possibly men, to report SGBV.

The rise of Arab female officers and the development of all-female police units have transformed how policing and community policing are performed. This area of study needs to be further explored to understand how these institutional transformations have impacted policing in the Arab world. In Morocco, female police officers are integrated into male police units and have a public presence in society. Moreover, they are likely to be seen as legitimate government actors no different than their male counterparts. For example, Moroccan female police officers were critical in ensuring that COVID-19 protocols were adhered to by conducting a sustained community engagement campaign that targeted families, women, and children. Women in Morocco have reached top positions in policing institutions and have been noted to have transformed policing administration, investigations, and outreach.

In Saudi Arabia, female police officers, for the first time, are policing the Hajj and Umrah services, in which millions of Muslims around the world attend. Female police officers have the same roles as men but provide services exclusively to female pilgrims (Reuters, 2021). In their study, Chu and Abdulla (2014) found that "female officers' attitudes in specialized female units promoted confidence, competence, and a positive self-efficacy." The unique reality of gender-segregated policing units in the Arab world not only expands the potential impact of police work but can also provide new and dynamic ways of understanding and conceptualizing policing as "specific conceptions of women in policing can act as a steppingstone to a more inclusive future" (Strobl, 2008). The ongoing research developments on Arab gender and policing will necessitate scholars of the Arab world to understand and reflect the diversity in the existing political, cultural, and religious arrangements. This can produce new and profound ways of understanding policing, gender, and crime in the Arab world.

The Future of Gender and Crime in the Arab World

The transdisciplinary efforts in Northern and Southern social science research on gender in the Arab world have developed leaps and bounds, producing dynamic insights and critical perspectives. However, the development of gender as a framework of study in the discipline of criminology is still in its infancy. Ultimately, the task of Arab criminology necessitates an active engagement with the established transdisciplinary theoretical frameworks to expand the disciplinary contours of Arab criminology. Doing so will produce new and dynamic ways of understanding crime and criminal justice systems in the Arab world, challenge Orientalist and colonial frameworks, and provide new theoretical and conceptual categories to contribute to the development of gender in Arab criminology.

References

Abadeer, A. S. Z. (2015). *Norms and gender discrimination in the Arab world* (1st ed.). Palgrave Macmillan.

Abulhab, S. D. (2011). *DeArabizing Arabia: Tracing western scholarship on the history of the Arabs and Arabic language and script*. Van Haren Publishing.

Aidi, H., Lynch, M., & Mampilly, Z. (2020). And the Twain Shall Meet: Connecting Africa and the Middle East. *Africa and the Middle East: Beyond the Divides*. Columbia School of International and Public Affairs.

Al-Badayneh, D. M. (2012). Violence against women in Jordan. *Journal of Family Violence*, 27(5), 369–379. https://doi.org/10.1007/s10896-012-9429-1

Al-Ghanim, K. (2013). The intellectual frameworks and theoretical limits of Arab feminist thought. *Contemporary Arab Affairs*, 6(1), 82–90. https://doi.org/10.1080/17550912.2012.748579

Ali, A. A., Yassin, K., & Omer, R. (2014). Domestic violence against women in Eastern Sudan. *BMC Public Health*, 14(1). https://doi.org/10.1186/1471-2458-14-1136

Alsaleh, M. A. (2015). Family violence in Syria. *Contemporary Perspectives in Family Research*, 99–127. https://doi.org/10.1108/s1530-353520150000009005

AlShehabi, O. H. (2019). Policing labour in empire: The modern origins of the Kafala sponsorship system in the Gulf Arab States. *British Journal of Middle Eastern Studies*, 48, 291–310. https://doi.org/10.1080/13530194.2019.1580183

Al-Warraq, A. (2019, June 4). The historic and systematic marginalization of Yemen's Muhamasheen community. *Sana'a Center for Strategic Studies*. https://sanaacenter.org/publications/analysis/7490

Arfaoui, K., & Moghadam, V. M. (2016). Violence against women and Tunisian feminism: Advocacy, policy, and politics in an Arab context. *Current Sociology*, 64(4), 637–653. https://doi.org/10.1177/0011392116640481

Aziz, S. (2021). Orientalism, empire, and the racial Muslim. *Overcoming Orientalism*, 221–244. https://doi.org/10.1093/oso/9780190054151.003.0009

Barberet, R., & Carrington, K. (2018). Globalizing feminist criminology: Gendered violence during peace and war. In *The Palgrave handbook of criminology and the global south* (pp. 821–845). Palgave Macmillan. https://doi.org/10.1007/978-3-319-65021-0_39

Bleakley, P., & Kehoe, T. J. (2021). Historical criminology as a field for interdisciplinary research and trans-disciplinary discourse. *History & Crime*, 125–141. https://doi.org/10.1108/978-1-80117-698-920211010

Brown, E., & Barganier, G. (2018). *Race and crime: Geographies of injustice* (1st ed.). University of California Press.
Bowling, B., & Phillips, C. (2003). Policing ethnic minority communities. In T. Newburn (Ed.), *Handbook of policing*. Cullompton: Willan.
Brown, J. A. C. (2019). *Slavery and Islam*. Oneworld Academic.
Carrington, K., Hogg, R., Scott, J., Sozzo, M., & Walters, R. (2018). *Southern criminology (New directions in critical criminology)* (1st ed.). Routledge.
Carrington, K., Hogg, R., & Sozzo, M. (2016). Southern criminology. *British Journal of Criminology*, 56(1), 1–20. https://doi.org/10.1093/bjc/azv083
Chafai, H. (2017). Contextualising street sexual harassment in Morocco: A discriminatory sociocultural representation of women. *The Journal of North African Studies*, 22(5), 821–840. https://doi.org/10.1080/13629387.2017.1364633
Charrad, M. M. (2011). Gender in the Middle East: Islam, state, agency. *Annual Review of Sociology*, 37(1), 417–437. https://doi.org/10.1146/annurev.soc.012809.102554
Christian, M. (2019). A global critical race and racism framework: Racial entanglements and deep and malleable whiteness. *Sociology of Race and Ethnicity*, 5(2), 169–185. https://doi.org/10.1177/2332649218783220
Chu, D. C., & Abdulla, M. M. (2014). Self-efficacy beliefs and preferred gender role in policing. *British Journal of Criminology*, 54(3), 449–468. https://doi.org/10.1093/bjc/azu010
Clark, C. J., Silverman, J. G., Shahrouri, M., Everson-Rose, S., & Groce, N. (2010). The role of the extended family in women's risk of intimate partner violence in Jordan. *Social Science & Medicine*, 70(1), 144–151. https://doi.org/10.1016/j.socscimed.2009.09.024
Connell, R. (2006). Northern theory: The political geography of general social theory. *Theory and Society*, 35(2), 237–264. https://doi.org/10.1007/s11186-006-9004-y
Connell, R. (2021). *Southern theory: The global dynamics of knowledge in social science* (1st ed.). Routledge.
Douki Dedieu, S., Ouali, U., Ghachem, R., Karray, H., & Issaoui, I. (2021). Violence against women in the Arab world: Eyes shut wide open. In *Handbook of healthcare in the Arab world* (pp. 207–255). Springer. https://doi.org/10.1007/978-3-030-36811-1_169
Egypt. (2017, May 8). *Understanding masculinities*. UN Women. https://imagesmena.org/en/egypt/
Elghossain, T., Bott, S., Akik, C., & Obermeyer, C. M. (2019). Prevalence of intimate partner violence against women in the Arab world: A systematic review. *BMC International Health and Human Rights*, 19(1). https://doi.org/10.1186/s12914-019-0215-5
El-Masri, S. (2021). ISIS's sexual slavery of Yazidi women and girls. *Human Rights in War*, 347–365. https://doi.org/10.1007/978-981-16-2116-1_14
Ennaji, M., & Sadiqi, F. (2011). *Gender and violence in the Middle East (UCLA Center for Middle East Development (CMED))* (1st ed.). Routledge.
ESCWA-UN. (2017). *Status of Arab women report 2017-violence against women: What is at stake?* https://archive.unescwa.org/file/66787/download?token=8T_2vB-Z

Fernandez, B. (2021). Racialised institutional humiliation through the *Kafala*. *Journal of Ethnic and Migration Studies*, *47*(19), 4344–4361. https://doi.org/10.1080/1369183x.2021.1876555

Freamon, B. (2021). *Possessed by the right hand the problem of slavery in Islamic law and Muslim cultures (Studies in Global Slavery)*. Brill.

Gaza: Israel's 'Open-Air Prison' at 15. (2022, June 14). *Human Rights Watch*. www.hrw.org/news/2022/06/14/gaza-israels-open-air-prison-15

Haddad, M. (2017). 'Victims of Rape and Law: How the Arab World Laws Protect the Rapist Not the Victim', *Jurist*. https://www.jurist.org/commentary/2017/05/mais-haddad-arab-world-laws-protect-the-rapist-not-the-victim/

Haj-Yahia, M. M., & Clark, C. J. (2013). Intimate partner violence in the occupied Palestinian territory: Prevalence and risk factors. *Journal of Family Violence*, *28*(8), 797–809. https://doi.org/10.1007/s10896-013-9549-2

Holt, M., & Jawad, H. A. (2013). Women, Islam, and resistance in the Arab world. London: Lynne Rienner Publishers.

Hasso, F. (2016). The sect-sex-police nexus and politics in Bahrain's pearl revolution. In F. Hasso & Z. Salime (Eds.), *Freedom without permission: Bodies and space in the Arab revolutions* (pp. 103–137). Duke University Press.

Holmes, A. A. (2018, April 19). What Egypt's racist campaign against Nubians reveals about Sissi's regime. *Washington Post*. www.washingtonpost.com/news/global-opinions/wp/2018/04/19/what-egypts-racist-campaign-against-nubians-reveals-about-sissis-regime/

Holt, M., & Jawad, H. A. (2013). *Women, Islam, and resistance in the Arab World*. London: Lynne Rienner Publishers.

Hopper, M. S. (2015). *Slaves of one master: Globalization and slavery in Arabia in the age of empire* (1st ed.). Yale University Press.

Hussein, N. A. (2018, March 2). Egyptian women look to boost presence in police force. *Al-Monitor: Independent, Trusted Coverage of the Middle East*. www.al-monitor.com/originals/2018/06/egypt-women-police-force-obstacles.html

Janmyr, M. (2016). Human rights and Nubian mobilisation in Egypt: Towards recognition of indigeneity. *Third World Quarterly*, *38*(3), 717–733. https://doi.org/10.1080/01436597.2016.1206454

Johansson-Nogués, E. (2013). Gendering the Arab spring? Rights and (in)security of Tunisian, Egyptian and Libyan women. *Security Dialogue*, *44*(5–6), 393–409. https://doi.org/10.1177/0967010613499784

Kalmar, I. D. (2013). *Early orientalism: Imagined Islam and the notion of sublime power*. Routledge.

Kamali, M. H. (2015). *The middle path of moderation in Islam: The Qur'anic principle of Wasatiyyah*. Oxford University Press.

Khattab, L., & Myrttinen, H. (2014, November 14). Gender, security, and SSR in Lebanon. *International Alert*, pp. 1–16.

King, S. J. (2019). Black Arabs and African migrants: Between slavery and racism in North Africa. *The Journal of North African Studies*, *26*(1), 8–50. https://doi.org/10.1080/13629387.2019.1670645

Kulczycki, A., & Windle, S. (2011). Honor killings in the Middle East and North Africa. *Violence against Women, 17*(11), 1442–1464. https://doi.org/10.1177/1077801211434127

Kulwicki, A. D. (2002). The practice of honor crimes: A glimpse of domestic violence in the Arab world. *Issues in Mental Health Nursing, 23*(1), 77–87. https://doi.org/10.1080/01612840252825491

LaFree, G., & Russell, K. K. (1993). The argument for studying race and crime. *Journal of Criminal Justice Education, 4*(2), 273–289. https://doi.org/10.1080/10511259300086141

Lafta, R. K., Al-Saffar, A. J., Eissa, S. A., & Al-Nuaimi, M. A. (2008). Gender-based violence: A study of Iraqi women. *International Social Science Journal, 59*(192), 309–316. https://doi.org/10.1111/j.1468-2451.2009.00700.x

Lebanon: Rising violence targets Syrian refugees. (2020, October 28). *Human Rights Watch*. www.hrw.org/news/2014/09/30/lebanon-rising-violence-targets-syrian-refugees

León, K. S. (2021). Critical criminology and race: Re-examining the whiteness of US criminological thought. *The Howard Journal of Crime and Justice, 60*(3), 388–408. https://doi.org/10.1111/hojo.12441

Lewis, B. (1976). *Islam and the Arab world: Faith, people, culture* (1st ed.). Random House.

Lewis, B. (1990). *Race and slavery in the Middle East: An historical enquiry* (New ed.). Oxford University Press.

Lockman, Z. (2004). *Contending visions of the Middle East: The history and politics of orientalism*. Cambridge University Press.

Lomazzi, V. (2020). Women's rights and Shari'a law in the mena region. *Migrants and Religion: Paths, Issues, and Lenses*, 231–250. https://doi.org/10.1163/9789004429604_009

Lori, N. & Kuzmova, Y. (2021, September). Who counts as "People of the Gulf"? Disputes over the Arab status of Zanzibaris in the UAE. In Aidi, H., Lynch, M. & Z. Mampilly (Eds.). *Racial formations in Africa and the Middle East; A Transregional Approach*. Project on Middle East Political Science (POMEPS) (44). pp. 107–114.

Mafu, L. (2019). The Libyan/trans-Mediterranean slave trade, the African Union, and the failure of human morality. *SAGE Open, 9*(1). https://doi.org/10.1177/2158244019828849

Mahadeen, E. (2017). 'The martyr of dawn': Femicide in Jordanian media. *Crime, Media, Culture: An International Journal, 13*(1), 41–54. https://doi.org/10.1177/1741659016643120

Mahdavi, P., & Sargent, C. (2011). Questioning the discursive construction of trafficking and forced labor in the United Arab Emirates. *Journal of Middle East Women's Studies, 7*(3), 6–35. https://doi.org/10.2979/jmiddeastwomstud.7.3.6

Makdisi, J. S. (2014). Huqouq almar'a: Feminist Thought and the Language of the Arab Women's Movement. In Makdisi, J.S. & Rafif, S. (Eds). Arab Feminisms: Gender and Equality in the Middle East. *Centre for Arab Unity Studies*, pp. 78–89.

Mazrui, A. (1969). The multiple marginalities of the Sudan. In *Violence and thought*. Longman's, Green and Co.

Mohanna, Z. (2006). Female criminality in the Arab world inspected from a Human Rights perspective. *Al Raida*, *8*(113), 50–54.

Odeh, L. A. (2010). Honor killings and the construction of gender in Arab societies. *American Journal of Comparative Law*, *58*(4), 911–952. https://doi.org/10.5131/ajcl.2010.0007

Ouassini, N., & Ouassini, A. (2020). Criminology in the Arab world: Misconceptions, nuances and future prospects. *The British Journal of Criminology*, *60*(3), 519–536.

Omi, M., & Winant, H. (1986). *Racial formation in the United States: From the 1960s to the 1990s*. Routledge.

Ouassini, A. (2021). We are all Amina Filali: Social media, civil society, and rape legislation reform in Morocco. *Women & Criminal Justice*, *31*(1), 77–82.

Ozcelik, B. (2021). Introduction: Confronting the legacy and contemporary iterations of racial politics in the Middle East. *Ethnic and Racial Studies*, *44*(12), 2155–2166. https://doi.org/10.1080/01419870.2021.1919312

Pepicelli, R. (2017). Rethinking gender in Arab nationalism: Women and the politics of modernity in the making of nation-states. Cases from Egypt, Tunisia and Algeria. *Oriente Moderno*, *97*(1), 201–219. https://doi.org/10.1163/22138617-12340145

Perea, J. F. (1997). The black/white binary paradigm of race: The "normal science" of American racial thought. *California Law Review*, *85*(5), 1213. https://doi.org/10.2307/3481059

Phillips, C., & Bowling, B. (2003). Racism, ethnicity and criminology. Developing minority perspectives. *British journal of criminology*, *43*(2), 269–290.

Phillips, C. (2003). Racism, ethnicity and criminology. Developing minority perspectives. *British Journal of Criminology*, *43*(2), 269–290. https://doi.org/10.1093/bjc/43.2.269

Phillips, C., Earle, R., Parmar, A., & Smith, D. (2020). Dear British criminology: Where has all the race and racism gone?. *Theoretical Criminology*, *24*(3), 427–446.

Qatar: Significant labor and Kafala reforms. (2020, November 4). *Human Rights Watch*. www.hrw.org/news/2020/09/24/qatar-significant-labor-and-kafala-reforms

Refaat, A., Dandash, K. F., Defrawi, M. H. E., & Eyada, M. (2001). Female genital mutilation and domestic violence among Egyptian women. *Journal of Sex & Marital Therapy*, *27*(5), 593–598. https://doi.org/10.1080/713846819

Reuters. (2021, July 21). Saudi women guard Mecca during hajj for first time. *Daily Sabah*. www.dailysabah.com/life/religion/saudi-women-guard-mecca-during-hajj-for-first-time

Said, E. (1978). Orientalism. Vintage Books.

Samiei, M. (2010). Neo-orientalism? The relationship between the West and Islam in our globalised world. *Third World Quarterly*, *31*(7), 1145–1160.

Sampson, R. J., Wilson, W. J., & Katz, H. (2018). Reassessing "toward a theory of race, crime, and urban inequality." *Du Bois Review: Social Science Research on Race*, *15*(1), 13–34. https://doi.org/10.1017/s1742058x18000140

Sato, M., & Moser, S. (2022). #FromFerguson2Gaza: Spatialities of protest in Black-Palestinian solidarity movements. *ACME: An International Journal for Critical Geographies*, *21*(1), 1–19.

Scott, J. G., Fa'avale, A., & Thompson, B. Y. (2018). What can southern criminology contribute to a post-race agenda? *Asian Journal of Criminology*, *13*(2), 155–173. https://doi.org/10.1007/s11417-017-9263-8

Sharkey, H. J. (2008). Arab identity and ideology in Sudan: The politics of language, ethnicity, and race. *African Affairs*, *107*(426), 21–43. https://doi.org/10.1093/afraf/adm068

Shiraz, M. S. (2016). The impact of education and occupation on domestic violence in Saudi Arabia. *International Journal of Social Welfare*, *25*(4), 339–346. https://doi.org/10.1111/ijsw.12214

Silverstein, P. A. (2002). The Kabyle myth. *From the Margins*, 122–155. https://doi.org/10.1215/9780822383345-005

Strobl, S. (2008). The women's police directorate in Bahrain. *International Criminal Justice Review*, *18*(1), 39–58. https://doi.org/10.1177/1057567708315642

Strobl, S. (2009). Policing housemaids: The criminalization of domestic workers in Bahrain. *British Journal of Criminology*, *49*(2), 165–183. https://doi.org/10.1093/bjc/azn071

Strobl, S. (2011). From colonial policing to community policing in Bahrain: The historical persistence of sectarianism. *International Journal of Comparative and Applied Criminal Justice*, *35*(1), 19–37. https://doi.org/10.1080/01924036.2011.535687

Stroble, S. (2006). Not so notorious: Crimes committed by Bahraini women in the Kingdom of Bahrain. *Al Raida*, *8*(113), 19–24.

Sutter, J. E. D. M. (2022, October 30). Slavery's last stand. *CNN*. https://edition.cnn.com/interactive/2012/03/world/mauritania.slaverys.last.stronghold/index.html

Tapper, R., & Tapper, N. (1992). Marriage honor and responsibility: Islamic and local models in the Mediterranean and the Middle East. *Cambridge Anthropology*, *16*(2), 3–21.

Telles, E. E. (2014). *Race in another America*. In Race in another America. Princeton University Press.

Tillous, M., & Lachenal, P. (2021). Can sexual violence be denounced without perpetrating class violence? Discussions on sexual harassment in Egypt. *ACME: An International Journal for Critical Geographies*, *20*(3), 231–240.

Tonnessen, L. (2014). When rape becomes politics: Negotiating Islamic law reform in Sudan. *Women's Studies International Forum*, *44*, 145–153. https://doi.org/10.1016/j.wsif.2013.12.003

Tunisia: Landmark step to shield women from violence. (2022, October 27). *Human Rights Watch*. www.hrw.org/news/2017/07/27/tunisia-landmark-step-shield-women-violence

UNSDG. (2021). Deep wounds: In the Arab Region, survivors of gender-based violence wonder where to turn. *UNSDG.UN.org*. https://unsdg.un.org/latest/stories/deep-wounds-arab-region-survivors-gender-based- violence-wonder-where-turn.

UN Women. (2013). *Study on ways and methods to eliminate sexual harassment in Egypt: Results/outcomes and recommendations. Cairo Demographic Center.* UN. www.peacewomen.org/node/90812

Yassine-Hamdan, N., & Strate, J. (2020). Gender inequality in the Arab world. *Contemporary Arab Affairs*, *13*(3), 25–50. https://doi.org/10.1525/caa.2020.13.3.25

Zaatari, Z. (2014). From Women's Rights to Feminism: The urgent need for an Arab feminist renaissance. In Makdisi, J.S. & Rafif, S. (Eds). Arab Feminisms: Gender and Equality in the Middle East. *Centre for Arab Unity Studies*, pp. 54–65.

Zaraket, S. (2020). The Kafala system: A story of modern slavery. *Lebanon Law Review*. https://lebanonlawreview.org/kafala/

5 Transnational Crime in the Arab World

Introduction

In the list of significant and growing threats to international security, transnational organized crime remains one of the United Nations' most pressing concerns. The globalized advances in communication, technology, transportation, and business have enhanced innovations in transnational crimes. The U.N. defines *transnational crime* as "offenses whose inception, perpetration and/or direct or indirect effects involve more than one country" (United Nations Office on Drugs and Crime, 2002, p. 4). The U.N. Convention against Transnational Organized Crime (2004) expounds that an organized criminal group consists of three or more people, exists for a certain period, works in concert to commit a crime punishable by at least four years, and conspires to obtain financial or material benefits directly or indirectly. Transnational criminal organizations engage in cybercrime, money laundering, fraud, illicit drug trafficking, human trafficking/smuggling, weapons trafficking, terrorism, and a range of other criminal activities.

As a phenomenon transcending territorial boundaries, the solutions for transnational crime require bilateral and multilateral strategies between states, regional actors, and the international community. When left unhandled, transnational crime undermines security, stability, development, governance, and the economy. The Arab world's location across North Africa and the Middle East situates the region in a strategic position as an exporter, intermediary, and destination for transnational crime. The past decades witnessed the intensification of terrorism, drug trafficking, and human smuggling/trafficking as three challenges to Arab criminal justice. Though many governments in the region have the means to combat these transnational crimes, the conflict-ridden failed states missing the conventional resources remain the most vulnerable.

This chapter examines the complex transnational crimes of terrorism, drug trafficking, and human smuggling/trafficking in the Arab world. These transnational crimes are ever evolving and, to various degrees, threaten the security of every Arab nation, regional actors, and the international community. The rapid expansion of these crimes within the Arab world exemplifies the mass mobilization and transmission of ideologies, illegal commodities, and people. The chapter specifically surveys the problems of terrorism and terrorist organizations, drug trafficking, and the smuggling and trafficking of people. Along with analyzing these transnational crimes, the chapter will evaluate the versatile responses and collaborative efforts from Arab governments. The conclusion identifies future research and substantiates how an Arab criminology subfield can productively situate and elucidate transnational crime in the Arab context.

Terrorism

The attacks on September 11 will always have a perennial impact on the world. The deaths of nearly 3,000 people from 78 different countries were caused by 19 terrorists from Arab countries. After two decades, the remnants of the attack persist. In the Arab world, the subsequent U.S. invasion of Afghanistan and Iraq, the War on Terror, the ensuing drone strikes, and the rise and fall of Islamic State engendered several crises and escalated political violence in the region. This section of the chapter will examine the transnational crime of terrorism in Arab states with a focus on government responses through manifold approaches ranging from international collaboration to localized alternative counterterrorism strategies. In the Arab Convention for the Suppression of Terrorism (1998, Article 1.2), the Arab League broadly defines terrorism as follows:

> Any act or threat of violence, whatever its motives or purposes, that occurs in the advancement of an individual or collective criminal agenda and seeking to sow panic among people, causing fear by harming them, or placing their lives, liberty or security in danger, or seeking to cause damage to the environment or to public or private installations or property or to occupying or seizing them, or seeking to jeopardize national resources.

Terrorism in the Arab world existed centuries before the attacks on September 11. During the Middle Ages, members of a Nizari Ismaeli sect (*al Nizariyyun*), known as the *al hashasheen* or the assassins, wreaked havoc on territories and kingdoms across the Middle East. The minority religious sect settled in Alamut Castle and utilized political murders against the surrounding Crusaders and Sunni Muslim Kingdoms to secure and retain their sovereignty (Garrison, 2003). In the past century, terrorism appeared in waves.

The early experiences with terrorism occurred in the British Mandate of Palestine. Groups like Menachem Begin's Irgun and Yitzhak Shamir's Lehi (Stern Gang) utilized terrorist attacks against the British government and the Arabs in Palestine with the objective of independence. The attack on the King David Hotel; the assassination of Lord Moyne, the British minister resident of the Middle East; the attempted assassination of Ernest Bevin, the British foreign secretary; along with the Deir Yassin and al-Dawayima massacres introduced modern terrorist strategies to the region.

During the Cold War, a new wave of terrorism emerged as the East–West polarization between the United States and the Soviet Union competed to influence the Arab world and other periphery countries. The Cold War, amalgamated with numerous nationalist, ethnic, and anti-colonial movements, accentuated left-wing extremism worldwide. Left-wing extremism proliferated through various Marxist/Leninist/Maoist movements and radical student organizations of the 1960s. Radicalized by American intervention in Vietnam, many students protested and eventually formed new terrorist groups modeled to be "the vanguard of the exploited and oppressed Third World" (Laqueur, 1999, p. 27). These left-wing extremist groups practiced terrorism by belonging to an exclusive organization with clearly defined objectives. The revolutionary ideas of Carlos Marighella, Che Guevarra, Frantz Fanon, and Mao Zedong inspired many of these left-wing extremists.

In the Arab world, pro-Western monarchies had an antagonistic relationship with Soviet-aligned Arab republics. Left-leaning pan-Arab movements flourished and successfully inspired the overthrow of monarchs in Egypt, Tunisia, Iraq, Libya, and Yemen. Many left-wing extremist groups "deny the legitimacy of the state and claim that the use of violence against it is morally justified" (Crenshaw, 1983, p. 2). The pro-Western Arab governments, with the aid of the United States and other Western governments, repressed all communist and left-wing movements. In the international arena, far-left militant Arab organizations partnered with international groups of the same ideologies. For example, the German Baader–Meinhof Gang worked with militant Palestinian groups, and others, like Carlos the Jackal, were part of the Popular Front for the Liberation of Palestine (PFLP) in its fight against Israeli occupation. The era was known for airplane hijackings, hostage-taking, bombings, and assassinations.

The fall of left-wing terrorism coincided with the rise of the next wave of terrorism. Islamist extremists aspired to remove the corrupt post-colonial rulers, eradicate Western influences from the Arab world, and reestablish an Islamic political, legal, and criminal justice system. Although Islamic activists were at the forefront of the anti-colonial struggle, the new post-colonial regimes perceived religious-based movements as a political threat. Egypt's president Nasser, for example, imprisoned and tortured members of the Muslim Brotherhood and had one of the leading members, Sayyid Qutb, executed. Islamist groups were suppressed yet oriented as a counterweight in the Arab world to the perceived threats from leftist ideologies. By the 1970s, the Iranian Revolution against the Shah became the blueprint for revolution against a corrupt Western-backed monarch setting off the Middle Eastern Cold War (Gause, 2014). Meanwhile, the Afghan War against the Soviet Union propagated Islamist extremism in the war on communism in what became known as the American Jihad (Parenti, 2001). The Central Intelligence Agency, Inter-Services Intelligence in Pakistan, and numerous Arab nations recruited, trained, and supplied volunteers and mercenaries from the Muslim world. Many fighters that joined the mujahideen were international Muslim extremists that would eventually drain and defeat the Soviet Union. In the end of the conflict, many Arab veterans of the Afghan War returned home to fuel armed conflicts that left thousands dead in Algeria, Egypt, Jordan, and other Arab states.

It was during this time in the 1990s that Al Qaeda became an international security threat. Founded by Osama bin Laden, the terrorist organization was initially based in Sudan and eventually relocated its headquarters to Afghanistan. Along with training fighters for future terrorist attacks, Al Qaeda bombed the U.S. embassies in East Africa and conducted a suicide attack on an American warship in Yemen. The attacks on September 11 were a watershed event in modern history. Most Arab nations offered support and stood in solidarity with the United States. However, the War on Terror and the Iraq War made terrorism worse in the region, and the Arab world experienced numerous attacks from Al Qaeda. Al Qaeda in Iraq utilized modern technology to recruit radical extremists from the Arab world to Iraq. The failure of the U.S. and Coalition forces to recognize Iraq's unique sectarian, political, tribal, and social dynamics aggregated the insurgency and the subsequent sectarian civil war that would lead to the Islamic State or Daesh. These failures to contain terrorism in Iraq contributed to the escalation of terrorism in other regions of the Arab world. The destruction of Iraq, Libya, Syria, and Yemen destabilized each regime and allowed terrorist groups to establish footholds across the Arab world.

In the early years of terrorism, Arab nations approached counterterrorism through targeted arrests, mass detentions, torture, and severe repression. Members of Al Qaeda that include al-Zawahiri, al-Zarqawi, al-Awlaki, and al-Baghdadi had all experienced the Arab world's repressive approach to terrorism. These conventional responses lead to a backlash that further radicalizes followers, increases member recruitment, and impedes any attempt by the government to counter extremist ideologies (Dragu & Polborn, 2014; Daxecker, 2017; Chakma, 2022). In the 1990s, Egypt led the effort with the Arab League to pass the Arab Convention for the Suppression of Terrorism.

The broad definition of terrorism, failure to incorporate safeguards for the rights of the accused, the impunity for perpetrators of certain crimes, and the potential for human rights violations were a few criticisms of the Convention (Amnesty International, 2002). By September 11, most Arab nations collectively passed various anti-terror legislation in two general trends. The first focused on domestic terrorism and placed international efforts in a subordinate role. The second passed after the Arab Spring focused on increasing authoritarian control in punishing dissent and quelling the spread of protests (Josua, 2021). Though these laws maintained a semblance of compliance with international norms, many regimes covertly participated in the CIA's extraordinary rendition programs and maintained secret detention facilities.

The Arab world has also applied innovative strategies and counterterrorism measures that require further research. There are cases in South Africa, Ireland, Peru, and Colombia of terrorism reconciliation as possible alternatives to retribution (Renner & Spencer, 2012). After the civil war in Algeria, President Bouteflika granted a general amnesty for Islamic militants and government forces. Despite the negative perceptions of victims (Zeraoulia, 2021), the amnesty brought about relative peace and security in the aftermath. The Yemeni government utilized Islamic scholars to conduct theological debates with low-level terrorists in prisons (Boucek et al., 2008). The debates created a space for Islamic scholars to convince terrorists to renounce violence. After a series of attacks from Al Qaeda, Saudi Arabia introduced religious rehabilitation programs for suspected terrorists (Al-Hadlaq, 2011). The programs provide counseling, re-education on extremists' interpretations of Islamic texts, recreational activities, and aftercare to reintegrate former terrorists back into society. These innovative approaches to terrorism are specific to each nation of the Arab world and were also implemented by the U.S. military in Iraq (Angell & Gunaratna, 2011) with lessons and opportunities for the current conflicts in Yemen, Libya, and Syria.

Drug Trafficking

Drug trafficking is the second major transnational crime plaguing the Arab world as a producer, shipment point, and market for various drugs. The geographic locations, spread across two continents, strategically position the Arab world into an essential role in drug trafficking. Luxurious cities like Dubai, for example, have become centers of illicit and drug activities (Page & Vittori, 2020), while trade in the region's seaports faces complications in container security (Zhao et al., 2017; Keshk, 2022). The illegal enterprises increased revenues for transnational gangs, mafias, terrorists, piracy, and other criminal organizations. Despite one of the lowest levels of pervasiveness globally, consumption in the region has increased along with the transmission of viral infections from injected drugs and shared drug equipment (Laher, 2021). The Arab world faces numerous challenges in the law, the criminal justice system, corruption, and the security of diverse terrain across 13 million square meters of land, sea, mountains, and deserts that disrupt the control of borders and enforcement of laws.

The MENA region has a long history of consuming hashish, opium, tobacco, qat, and coffee (Ram, 2022). Every country in the Arab world produces and consumes disparate drugs. Morocco's Rif region and Lebanon's Beqaa Valley have long supplied MENA and Europe with a steady supply of cannabis. The Gulf is currently facing an addiction crisis related to amphetamine-type of stimulants. Among the youth in Saudi Arabia, the amphetamine fenethylline, known as Captagon, has become quite popular. Somalia and Yemen continue to chew qat in long celebrated male social circles. According to Kraehe (2018), drug trafficking in the region has three general responses from drug-producing states. The first is direct state participation in the opium and cannabis trade to benefit the regime, as was practiced by Syria in the 1980s and 1990s. The second is indirect participation to benefit state clients. Libya, in the mid-1990s, imported cocaine to support militant groups in Latin America. Finally, Kraehe (2018) identifies the response of tolerance for economic benefits. As one of the largest producers of cannabis in the world, Morocco tolerates the cultivation of cannabis since it has helped many families out of extreme poverty and significantly contributed to the economies of Morocco's Northern cities. However, the main concern in the region is the nexus of narco-terrorism. There have been links between terrorist organizations and drugs in Lebanon, Syria, Iraq, Somalia, and the Sahel.

In response to drug trafficking, most Arab governments privately collect data on all information on the production, trafficking, and consumption of drugs but refuse to share information with the public. The response to drug trafficking ranges from harsh punishments in the Gulf to Morocco's legalization of cannabis for medical, cosmetic, and industrial purposes (Tinasti, 2020; McDowall, 2022). Despite these wide-ranging approaches, the region's adverse political conditions and security challenges will likely increase drug-related crime (Barzoukas, 2017). Governments and NGOs need to gather and openly share data on drug production and consumption to understand the levels of MENA's drug trafficking. The on-the-ground reality is that even in the most resourceful nations, drug trafficking is difficult to disrupt completely. Nevertheless, like terrorism, repression, punitive punishment, and social stigma cannot be the only solutions for the region's drug problems and alternative approaches need further exploration.

Human Trafficking

The crimes of human trafficking and smuggling are some of the most urgent transnational challenges in the Arab world. According to the U.N. Protocol to Prevent, Suppress and Punish Trafficking in Persons, human trafficking is the recruitment, transportation, transfer, harboring, or receipt of persons by threatening or forcing, deceiving, coercing, and abusing power or of a position of vulnerability with the purpose of exploitation (U.N., 2000). Unlike when trafficked persons must generate money for their traffickers, human smuggling relates to the violation of immigration laws, with the relationship between smugglers and migrants ending once an individual arrives at their destination (Kleemans & Smit, 2014).

The U.S. invasion of Iraq, the War on Terror, the aftermath of the Arab Spring, and the ensuing conflicts in Syria, Libya, Somalia, and Yemen produced thousands of migrants and refugees moving away from the region through Syria, Turkey, and Greece. The Syrian conflict, in particular, has displaced more than half of the country's pre-war population of 23 million, making the refugees vulnerable to forced labor and sex trafficking in Lebanon, Jordan, Iraq, and Turkey (U.S. State Department, 2022). Traffickers and smugglers in the Mediterranean have ruthlessly exploited refugees to make a fortune smuggling and trafficking those seeking a safe passage to Europe. Similarly, the North African coast is one of the popular destinations for migrants from sub-Saharan Africa and the Maghreb attempting to reach the southern coasts of Europe. Smugglers exploit the migrants and refugees by charging exuberant fees or subjecting them to forced labor or prostitution. In post-Gaddafi Libya, migrants pursuing a route into southern Italy were targeted by criminal organizations and militia groups for slavery and slave trading (Lewis et al., 2021).

The Gulf and the Levant have become destinations for predominantly Asian domestic and migrant workers seeking employment. The migrants arrive to Jordan, Lebanon, and the Gulf under the network of the *kafala* system. The *kafala* system is an approach to immigration that forfeits the regulation of migrants from the government to private citizens and corporations. The *kafala* system originates from the British colonial system of organizing and monitoring foreign workers with the help of residents (AlShehabi, 2021). The *kafala* system is one that Ruhs (2013, p. 98) describes as "an employer-led, large-scale guest worker program that is open to admitting migrant workers, but at the same time restrictive in terms of the rights granted to migrants after admission."

The response to human trafficking and smuggling in the Arab world varies by country. The Global Organized Crime Index ranks Libya, the U.A.E., and Yemen among the worst five countries for human trafficking while ranking Iraq and Syria as the third worst in human smuggling (Miles, 2021). There were attempted reforms in the *kafala* system, with countries passing legislation to combat human trafficking and smuggling. Nevertheless, more is needed, and activists argue for stringent legislation to protect migrants and assist police in enforcing laws. The countries in the region destroyed by incessant conflict will continue to struggle with human trafficking and smuggling. These nations will require aid from regional and international actors to clamp down on transnational crimes.

Arab and International Collaboration

In line with the objectives of Arab criminology, the Arab world has resorted to and relied on the Arab League to discuss, evaluate, and confront terrorism, drug trafficking, and human trafficking/smuggling. The magnitude of these transnational crimes requires bilateral and multilateral approaches due to the region's ample political, economic, and social predicaments. The porous borders, strategic location, economic and development disparities, and corruption make a unilateral approach unviable. In fact, in some failed states, the black-market economy is the only way to subsist. Arab states and non-governmental organizations, with the support of the international community, are all collaborating to produce a solution to strengthen internal and regional security. Transnational crimes have provided a path from which Arab states can mutually coordinate, invest in local criminal justice systems, and collectively support regional institutional capacity.

In counter-terrorism, the Arab League has worked with member states to sign the Arab Strategy to Combat terrorism (1997) and the Arab Convention for the Suppression of Terrorism (1998). These approach terrorism in a manner that suits the region by using international law and tenets of Islamic law. The Convention also discerns between conventional Northern approaches to terrorism and a Southern definition "affirming the right of peoples to combat foreign occupation and aggression by whatever means, including armed struggle, in order to liberate their territories and secure their right to self-determination, and independence" (League of Arab States, 1998, Preamble). The preamble emphasizes the distinction between legitimate armed struggle and terrorism. The Arab League has also applied the Regional Program for the Arab States to Prevent and Combat Crime, Terrorism, and Health to help the government combat transnational crime and corruption in compliance with international human rights standards and the rule of law (UNODC, 2021). An Arab criminological framework also shapes the legislation passed regarding terrorism financing. The *hawala* money transfers and other informal methods of moving money across the Arab world have reinforced the importance of a regional Arab approach in establishing financial intelligence units to investigate and shut down the unlicensed money-transfer centers that are often built on tribal and movement networks that move beyond the nation-state.

Along with these Conventions, Saudi Arabia has proposed an Arab joint military force to confront terrorism (Sheira & Ammash, 2015) and an Islamic Military Counterterrorism Alliance of over 41 Muslim countries (Al-Ghafli, 2018). The military coalitions would train, equip, share information, and strategize campaigns against terrorist organizations. In law enforcement, the Arab Interior Ministers Council (AIMC) and the Arab League liaised with INTERPOL to collect biometric data on terrorists in Libya and Iraq and successfully captured 12 terrorist suspects attempting to cross maritime borders in the Mediterranean (Interpol, 2019).

In the 1990s, the Arab League adopted the Arab Convention against Illicit Traffic in Narcotic Drugs and Psychotropic Substances to encourage cooperation between Arab states in reducing drug trafficking. In the Arab world's contemporary war on drugs, the Arab League has primarily worked with the United Nations Office on Drugs and Crime (UNODC). The Arab League has used the UNODC's recommendations to respond to illicit drug trafficking under the Regional Programme for the Arab States to Prevent and Combat Crime, Terrorism, and Health Threats. The UNODC program has advocated for the improvement of legislation; the collection, analysis, and sharing of data on trafficking routes and criminal activities; the support/ special training for law enforcement agencies investigating transnational crime and working the borders; enhancement of the criminal justice system to respond adequately; and increasing cooperation between Arab states (UNODC, 2021). In the resourceful countries of the Gulf, the Gulf Criminal Information Center to Combat Drugs (GCC-CICCD) is the nexus for law enforcement agencies combatting drug trafficking in each GCC country.

The Arab League has also guided efforts to combat human trafficking and smuggling among Arab states. In the early 2000s, the Arab League created the Anti-Human Trafficking Coordinating Unit to coordinate between Arab states and monitor regional trends. The Council of Arab Ministers of Justice and the Council of Arab Ministers of Interior built on the former efforts by adopting the Arab Guiding Law on Human Trafficking to assist Arab states in drafting national anti-trafficking legislation. Similarly, the Council of Arab Ministers adopted the Comprehensive Arab Strategy for Combatting Trafficking in Human Beings with recommendations that Arab States: (1) criminalize all forms of human trafficking; (2) guarantee efficiency in the criminal process; (3) work on prevention; (4) protest victims; (5) promote regional and international cooperation; (6) strengthen national institutional capacity; (7) update laws of human trafficking; and (8) coordinate with the

Arab state (Gui, 2013). An annual conference in Doha, Qatar, assembles the Arab League, the UNODC regional office, and various delegates to discuss the Arab Initiative for Building National Capacities for Combating Human Trafficking. This initiative promotes regional and international cooperation with numerous training workshops for attendees to build capacity across the Arab world.

Conclusion

The Arab world faces numerous challenges in preventing transnational crime due to corruption, inadequacies in criminal justice, extensive borders across diverse terrains, as well as the region's ongoing civil wars, conflicts, and failed states. To reduce transnational crime in the region, the practices of good governance, the rule of law, and accountability can gain legitimacy and improve criminal justice in the Arab world. Countries with ample resources are striving to reform and improve these practices. The Gulf Cooperation Council Police (GCCPOL) has set high standards through several initiatives to strengthen security cooperation and combat transnational crime. The Arab League and the UNODC's Regional Program for the Arab States' emphasis on strengthening criminal justice and the coordination between the Arab Interior Ministers' Council have been a significant success in matters of law enforcement, national security, and transnational crime. More importantly, the chapter demonstrates the centrality of Arab criminology as a pertinent approach to assessing transnational crimes. Arab states recognize the commonalities and must work closely to address transnational crimes. Transnational crime within Arab criminology requires further research from a Southern Arab perspective, especially when evaluating prevention and alternative approaches. The research on crime remains sensitive, and research on transnational issues is complex. Arab legislatures and local criminal justice systems need to pass and enforce legislation that protects victims and supports an Arab regional approach to mobilize resources against these crimes. There is a need to support victims, use the media to inform the public, work with NGOs and civil society organizations, and apply the latest technology.

Finally, the chapter identifies the potential research prospects for the subdiscipline of Arab criminology. What is important to note in this brief discussion on transnational crimes are the efforts made by Arab states to actively engage it. More importantly, the chapter demonstrates Arab criminology as pertinent to producing research from an Arab perspective, especially in constructing localized approaches and prevention mechanisms to regional criminological questions and issues in the Arab world.

References

Al-Ghafli, A. (2018). The Islamic military alliance to fight terrorism: Structure, mission, and politics. *Journal of Regional Security*, *12*(2), 157–185.

Al-Hadlaq, A. (2011). Terrorist rehabilitation: The Saudi experience. In R. Gunaratna, J. Jerard, & L. Rubin (Eds.), *Terrorist rehabilitation and counter-radicalisation: New approaches to counter-terrorism* (pp. 59–69). Routledge.

AlShehabi, O. H. (2021). Policing labour in empire: The modern origins of the Kafala sponsorship system in the Gulf Arab States. *British Journal of Middle Eastern Studies*, *48*(2), 291–310.

Amnesty International. (2002, January 9). *The Arab convention for the suppression of terrorism: A serious threat to human rights.* Amnesty International Publications. www.amnesty.org/en/documents/ior51/001/2002/en/

Angell, A., & Gunaratna, R. (2011). *Terrorist rehabilitation: The US experience in Iraq.* CRC Press.

Barzoukas, G. (2017). *Drug trafficking in the MENA* (Vol. 29). European Institute for Security Studies, Brief.

Boucek, C., Beg, S., & Horgan, J. (2008). Opening up the Jihadi debate: Yemen's committee for dialogue. In T. Bjørgo & J. Horgan (Eds.), *Leaving terrorism behind* (pp. 181–192). Routledge.

Chakma, A. (2022). Does state repression stimulate terrorism? A panel data analysis on South Asia. *Journal of Policing, Intelligence and Counter Terrorism*, 1–18.

Crenshaw, M. (1983). *Terrorism, legitimacy, and power: The consequences of political violence.* Wesleyan University Press.

Daxecker, U. (2017). Dirty hands: Government torture and terrorism. *Journal of Conflict Resolution*, *61*(6), 1261–1289.

Dragu, T., & Polborn, M. (2014). The rule of law in the fight against terrorism. *American Journal of Political Science*, *58*(2), 511–525.

Garrison, A. (2003). Terrorism: The nature of its history. *Criminal Justice Studies: A Critical Journal of Crime, Law and Society*, *16*(1), 39–52.

Gause, F. G., III (2014). Beyond sectarianism: The new Middle East cold war. *Brookings Doha Center Analysis Paper*, *11*, 1–27.

Gui, C. (2013). Arab League combating human trafficking. *Università degli Studi di Padova Centro di Ateneo per i Diritti Umani.* https://unipd-centrodirittiumani.it/en/schede/Arab-League-combating-human-trafficking/300

Interpol. (2019, December 11). Arab world plays vital role in global security. *Interpol Chief.* www.interpol.int/en/News-and-Events/News/2019/Arab-world-plays-vital-role-in-global-security-INTERPOL-Chief

Josua, M. (2021). What drives diffusion? Anti-terrorism legislation in the Arab Middle East and North Africa. *Journal of Global Security Studies*, 1–15. https://doi.org/10.1093/jogss/ogaa049

Keshk, A. M. (2022). *Maritime security of the Arab Gulf states: Analysis of current threats, confrontation mechanisms, and future challenges.* Springer Nature.

Kleemans, E. R., & Smit, M. (2014) Human smuggling, human trafficking, and exploitation in the sex industry. In L. Paoli (Ed.), *Oxford handbook of organized crime* (pp. 381–401). Oxford University Press.

Kraehe, G. C. (2018). Contested terrain: The new geography of drug trafficking in North Africa and the Sahel since the Arab Spring. *Small Wars Journal.* https://smallwarsjournal.com/jrnl/art/contested-terrain-new-geography-drug-trafficking-north-africa-and-sahel-arab-spring

Laher, I. (Ed.). (2021). *Handbook of healthcare in the Arab world.* Springer Nature.

Laqueur, W. (1999). *The new terrorism: Fanaticism and the arms of mass destruction.* Oxford University Press.

Lewis, A., Amulega, S., & Langmia, K. (2021). "Arab Spring" or Arab winter: Social media and the 21st-century slave trade in Libya. In *Routledge handbook of African media and communication studies* (pp. 181–191). Routledge.

McDowall, A. (2022, October 5). Morocco issues first permits for cannabis production. *Reuters.* www.reuters.com/world/africa/morocco-issues-first-permits-cannabis-production-2022-10-05/

Miles, H. (2021, October 6). Middle East and North Africa top organized crime report. *Fair Observer.* www.fairobserver.com/region/middle_east_north_africa/hugh-miles-global-organized-crime-index-2021-middle-east-north-africa-news-66578/

Page, M., & Vittori, J. (2020, July 7). Dubai's role in facilitating corruption and global illicit financial flows. *Carnegie Endowment for International Peace.* https://carnegieendowment.org/2020/07/07/dubai-s-role-in-facilitating-corruption-and-global-illicit-financial-flows-pub-82180

Parenti, C. (2001). America's jihad: A history of origins. *Social Justice, 28*(85), 31–38.

Ram, H. (2022). Middle East drug cultures in the long view. In P. Gootenberg (Ed.), *The Oxford handbook of global drug history* (pp. 230–248). Oxford University Press.

Renner, J., & Spencer, A. (Eds.). (2012). *Reconciliation after terrorism: Strategy, possibility or absurdity?* Routledge.

Ruhs, M. (2013). *The price of rights: Regulating international labor migration.* Princeton University Press.

Sheira, O., & Ammash, M. (2015). *Arab league summit report* (no. 10). Global Political Trends Center Istanbul Kultur University.

The League of Arab States. (1998). *The Arab Convention for the suppression of terrorism.* www.unodc.org/images/tldb-f/conv_arab_terrorism.en.pdf

Tinasti, K. (2020). Drug use, policies and prohibition in Muslim countries. In D. R. Bewley-Taylor & K. Tinasti (Eds.), *Research handbook on international drug policy* (pp. 145–162). Edward Elgar Publishing.

United Nations. (2000). *Protocol to prevent, suppress and punish trafficking in persons, especially women and children, supplementing the United Nations Convention against transnational organized crime.* www.ohchr.org/en/instruments-mechanisms/instruments/protocol-prevent-suppress-and-punish-trafficking-persons

United Nations Office on Drugs and Crime. (2002). *Global program against transnational organized crime: Results of pilot survey of forty selected organized criminal groups in sixteen countries.* www.undoc.org/unodc/en/organized_crime.html

United Nations Office on Drugs and Crime. (2004). *United Nations Convention against transnational organized crime and the protocols thereto.* www.unodc.org/unodc/en/organized-crime/intro/UNTOC.html

United Nations Office on Drugs and Crime. (2021). *Regional programme for the Arab States (2016-2021)*. www.unodc.org/romena/uploads/documents/Regional Programmes/Regional_Programme_for_the_Arab_States_2016-2021.pdf

United States State Department. (2022). *2022 trafficking in persons report: Syria*. www.state.gov/reports/2022-trafficking-in-persons-report/syria/

Zeraoulia, F. (2022). National reconciliation in Algeria from a bottom-up approach: Analysing victims' narratives. *The Journal of North African Studies*, *27*(5), 862–893.

Zhao, X., Yan, H., & Zhang, J. (2017). A critical review of container security operations. *Maritime Policy & Management*, *44*(2), 170–186.

6 Moving Forward

Establishing the Parameters of an Arab Criminology

Criminology is still in its infancy in the Arab world. While there have been tremendous developments, the incorporation and adoption of Arab criminology still has ways to go (Ouassini & Ouassini, 2020). The absence of a modern criminological tradition in the Arab world reveals that many scholars, politicians, and academics still wield a minimal understanding of what criminology is and its potential to expand and break through the grip of Orientalist and traditional Islamic legal frameworks that govern crime, criminality, and justice administration. Nevertheless, the potential development of Arab criminology is considerable as the Arab world has a long history of social scientific research and theory development in both the Islamic intellectual traditions and the Northern social sciences that can foster the integration of criminology in Arab universities and public security institutions (Sabagh & Ghazalla, 1986; Ibrahim, 1997; Abdul-Jabar, 2014; Ouassini & Ouassini, 2020). Arab academics and scholars in and outside of the Arab world who conduct research and write about crime, criminality, and criminal justice can build on other established disciplines, including anthropology, sociology, political science, and law, to challenge theoretical orientations in their respective specializations and partake in the development of Arab criminology as an academic discipline of study (Ouassini & Ouassini, 2020).

While the development of Arab criminology, including its acceptance and expansion, necessitates that we acknowledge that at its core is the Northern discipline, we maintain that its importation into the Arab world will produce new theoretical and methodological frameworks specific to the region and national settings (Hanafi & Arvanitis, 2016). Certainly, this must be taken into consideration as Arab criminology "must be looked at from the viewpoint of the developing country. Ideas are often exported as manufactured goods, and as a result is often disastrous to third world countries" (Jones, 1981, p. 166). We envision Arab criminology will reflect the lived realities of the Arab world while engaging with the 'criminologies' of the North and South as a starting point in theoretical and methodological development. In doing so, we contend that Arab criminological scholarship must develop localized theoretical orientations while simultaneously testing Northern and Southern criminological theories (Liu, 2017, p. 75) to understand their potential viability and applicability in the Arab world (Ouassini & Ouassini, 2020). Consequently, this will require the testing of theoretical orientations across the Arab world to "evaluate their feasibility; and generalizing them to a broader scope" (Liu, 2017, p. 77) as well as to develop standards for peer-reviewed scientific research, evaluate programs/policies, and maintain a robust data infrastructure and pipeline for criminologists to employ (Hanafi & Arvanitis, 2016).

As outlined throughout the chapters, the unique historical, political, religious, and cultural similarities across the Arab world not only forge a subdiscipline distinct from other criminological area studies while also acknowledging the similarities. The stark differences between and among the Arab nations that will produce locally specific approaches, analysis, and findings. For example, Alotaibi et al. (2019) seminal article exploring motor vehicle theft in Saudi Arabia reveals how cultural and religious differences in Saudi Arabia necessitate the development of localized environmental criminological models that are different from Northern and Southern criminological frameworks. The authors provide several examples to account for these distinct differences including the use of the Hijri calendar (Islamic calendar), which is based on the Prophet Muhammed's migration from Mecca to Medina and the lunar cycle, the five daily prayers in which shops are required to be closed during such periods, the Month of Ramadan and the accompanying fast, the two Eid Festivals, and the alternative weekend schedule which for many Arab nations includes Friday, to accommodate the weekly Friday Muslim congregational prayer. These dependent variables Alotaibi et al. (2019) maintain are necessary to engage and employ in order to conduct research when studying environmental crimes in the Arab world.

Additionally, the context-specific framework employed in the development of Arab criminology needs to consider the integral role of formal and informal organizations, tribal institutions, charismatic and religious personalities, civil society, and movement mobilizations on the criminal justice systems in the Arab world (Wardak, 2019; Ouassini, 2019). For instance, in Iraq, like in many other Arab nations, nearly 75% of the Iraqi population belongs to or identifies with a tribe; it is thus pivotal to understand the role of these non-state actors in the varied Arab criminal justice systems and how this impacts citizens' conceptualization of criminal justice legitimacy (Bobseine, 2019, p. 3). For example, in Jordan and Yemen, tribal communities still enforce the customary practice of *al jala* (banishment) in their informal criminal justice processes. The *al jala* requires the offender and their innocent family members to depart their tribe in an unresolved case to limit the potential of armed revenge and honor killings, especially if the victim was from another tribe. Often, the offender and their families are not allowed back into the tribe until the dispute is solved and a resolution is in place. These informal processes safeguard and prevent communal and tribal violence and integrate traditional reparative measures outside the state's power and authority (Alibeli et al., 2011, p. 47).

Coupled with the environmental and tribal differences between the Arab world and Northern and Southern nations, there are several areas Arab criminology can inform and expand on, including Islamic law, especially the hybrid criminal justice models established throughout the Arab world. Other areas include Islamic models for restorative justice, culture, family, race, ethnicity, gender, transnational movements, internal colonialism, Arab transnational media, cybercrime, and violence in the context of ongoing civil conflicts, terrorism, and occupations. Pursuing these area studies within a criminological framework will produce new and profound questions, grounded theoretical models, and new methodologies that can sift through Orientalist and Islamophobic preconceptions and Northern superimposed disciplinary frameworks to formulate Arab criminology.

Arab Criminology: Between the Northern, Southern, and Decolonial Traditions?

Central to the conversation surrounding the development of Arab criminology is where we position the subdiscipline between Northern, Southern, and decolonial approaches. As the previous chapters have established, Arab criminologists must consider the role of European colonialism in constructing modern Arab states. The remnants of European colonization are the hybrid legal models that define contemporary Arab criminal justice systems. By and large, this necessitates that Arab scholars recognize that the systems they are integrated into and work in will require Northern, Southern, and decolonial theoretical tools and methodologies to understand, support, or deconstruct Arab criminology. For example, in many post-colonial Arab states, the French civil code, which encouraged underage girls to 'marry their rapists' so men could avoid prosecution, is still enforced (Mesbahi, 2018). Morocco's effort to challenge and repeal the remnant of this French colonial law (Article 475) included activists, transnational feminists, Islamic legal scholars, and local criminal justice actors (Ouassini, 2019).

Thus, it is crucial that Arab criminology be cognizant of the on-the-ground lived realities of the Arab world and not fall into an iron cage of criminological cliques that have fortified disciplinary boundaries. Acknowledging these variables, including history, colonization, empire, decolonization, globalization, and transnationalism(s), which impact the very definition of the Arab world, will need to engage with and break through the iron cage. Arab criminology can potentially fill this gap by challenging the "ethnocentrism that characterizes criminology" (Moosavi, 2019, p. 259) by moving beyond the embedded Orientalist philosophies. Accordingly, this will further guarantee a paradigm shift that will potentially "indigenize" Arab criminology to support the development of theories and conceptual frameworks that focus on the individual and collective Arab nation. Moosavi (2019) further suggests that criminology(s) interrogates "their philosophical, epistemological and ontological premises" (261), especially as they evolve and expand. Undoubtedly, Moosavi's assertion is especially important as it questions whether Arab criminology or any subsequent criminologies can become truly independent of their Northern criminological roots. The realities of globalization, authoritarianism, neo-liberalism, and the post-colonial structure of Arab states suggest we are too far gone. Disentanglement between Northern criminology and Indigenous Arab criminology will presumably not happen any time soon as Arab criminologists will need a base and foothold to build off to institutionalize the discipline in the Arab world.

Furthermore, the Arab world is steeped in Northern systems, methods, and processes, including the "hybrid legal systems in the region (which) demonstrate the enduring exchanges between Arab and Western criminology" (Ouassini & Ouassini, 2020, p. 11). Additionally, the university setting from which Arab criminology will be housed in the Arab world is often modeled and/or influenced by American and European university curricular structures (Bagader, 1997). Including a curriculum that primarily represents and is fortified in Western intellectual traditions, especially in the social sciences, will play a foundational role in developing Arab criminology. In addition, access to the Northern and Southern social scientific literature is usually the standard that most social scientists in the Arab world reference, as most scientific publications are not translated into Arabic (Hanafi & Arvanitis, 2016). For most universities across the Arab world, the lingua franca is often superimposed by the state and tends to be either French or English (Bagader, 1997, p. 64).

In the field of sociology, a discipline closely related to criminology, most of the Arab scholars of the 20th century wrote and published from positivist, structural-functionalist, and Marxist frameworks (Sabagh & Ghazalla, 1986; Ibrahim, 1997; Abdul-Jabar, 2014). As Abdul Al-Jabbar (2014, p. 503) contends, Arab sociological thought "is a mere replica of the old ideological dividing lines inhabiting the minds of Arab intellectuals, Marxists, National Socialists, Arabists. Islamists, and, to some extent, Liberals, as well." Thus, we expect Arab criminology will initially reflect the Northern traditions. However, as the discipline becomes more entrenched and local scholars engage with and conduct on-the-ground research, we expect more publications by Arab scholars in Arabic, English, and French coupled with new-hybrid theoretical and methodological orientations. As Moosavi (2019) warns regarding Asian and Southern criminology, it is essential to acknowledge the realities and struggles that exist pertaining to knowledge production in the post-colonial Arab world, and thus, to claim an 'authentic voice' one must acknowledge and accept the hybrid realities of the post-colonial Arab world. In doing so, scholars can avoid 'reproducing the imperialist arrogance' that Arab criminology claims to decenter (Moosavi, 2019, p. 264) by collectively acknowledging the influences of all criminologies (Carrington et al., 2016).

Challenges of an Arab Criminology

The rise of Arab criminology will have to contend with several challenges that "will vary by individual regimes with each national context demarcating matters that are off-limits and others that are tolerated" (Ouassini & Ouassini, 2020). While there are many similarities across the 22 Arab states, the differences are also stark and can lead to many contentions of what constitutes Arab criminology when conducting research and theoretical development. For example, criminology in Mauritania and its predominantly tribal and rural communities with their differing conceptions of race, ethnicity, and gender will be vastly different in form and analysis than in Tunisia, which historically has had more direct and widespread experience with urbanization and modernization.

Secondly, understanding the effects of authoritarian states on Arab criminology will be especially demanding, particularly in fragmented states like Syria, conflict-ridden states like Somalia and Libya, and military dictatorships like Egypt. In these contexts, not only is research a difficult endeavor, it is often tied to the interests of the ruling elite. Arab governments' hegemonic control over university institutions and especially the social sciences is a challenge that Arab criminologists must face head-on as "social sciences are a prime target; they are locked into academic institutions that are fully subsumed under central educational command and monopoly, devoid of the internationally recognized standards of intellectual freedoms" (Abdul-Jabar, 2014, p. 503). This is especially important to consider as criminal justice institutions have historically facilitated Arab governments' dominance over its territorial boundaries and populations. In such authoritarian contexts, Arab governments can potentially use Arab criminology to sustain control and power over both state and society. This is further evidenced by the fact that Arab authoritarian states and their accompanying criminal justice systems are locally and globally perceived to be directly connected to and inextricably linked with inhumane and vulgar criminal justice practices, including torture and state-imposed human rights violations in correctional facilities, police brutality, corruption, and the lack of due process.

Thirdly, another challenge facing the development of Arab criminology is the minimal work that has been done on crime, criminality, and criminal justice in the Arab world. This indicates that we do not have a succinct data infrastructure to sustain theoretical development outside of Western disciplinary boundaries of political science, anthropology, sociology, and Islamic studies.

Fourth, the lack of access to journal databases for Arab social scientists in the Arabic, English, and French languages limits the potential growth and expansion of Arab criminology as it confines intellectual exchange and exposure to new emerging ideas and studies. This is coupled with the limited venues available to publish criminal justice research, questionable policies shaping academic freedom, lack of funding infrastructure for research, and complex and challenging research conditions (Ouassini & Ouassini, 2020). Finally, most studies published in the Arab world dealing with crime, criminality, and criminal justice are primarily descriptive studies that rarely include theoretical frameworks outside the Northern criminological tradition or the established Islamic legal frameworks. This reflects the general status of scientific research in the Arab world, which often does not have the funding available for research endeavors, a viable and transparent data infrastructure, or is not open to questions surrounding academic freedom (Bagader, 1997, p. 67).

Arab Criminology Data – Data for an Arab Criminology

One of the critical issues that must be considered when addressing the development of Arab criminology is the question of data and data collection in the Arab world. Unlike the documented data infrastructure present in Northern criminology, the lack of data systems in the Arab world can significantly impact the development of Arab criminology. Moreover, the Arab world does not have the same traditions in translating data-driven research to construct policy. While some Arab nations have comprehensive data collection and reporting agencies, the reality is that the crime data used and compiled is highly manipulated, regulated, politicized, and often restricted. Arab criminologists must engage with Northern and Southern criminological institutions to aid in the development of the Arab world's criminological data infrastructure. As a result, this can potentially aid Arab government bodies and criminal justice agencies to develop and sustain data infrastructures to support on the ground criminological research.

The viability of Arab criminology will depend on the active collection and storage of the data and the establishment of a robust and transparent data infrastructure, including data pipelines to streamline access to criminal justice scholars, practitioners, civil society activists, and government agencies. While each Arab nation has a specific policy dealing with the data collected from their populations, in the case of Arab criminology, Arab criminologists must work with and aid criminal justice agencies to capture data points that measure crime and criminality at the national, city, neighborhood, community, and household levels (Bennett & Lynch, 1996, p. 20). Just like the other criminologies, the collected data should capture all criminal incidents, including the crime's context and associations, the victim and offender identities, and relative variables (Bennett & Lynch, 1996, p. 20).

Additionally, this includes developing victimization surveys to capture crimes that are not officially reported, especially in the Arab world, where many cultural and gendered criminal activities limit the possibility of reporting critical information to authorities. The availability of such a survey will reveal more comparable data to explain the reality of crime and criminality while also informing public policy. An Arab criminological approach has the potential to produce new and dynamic mediums to collect criminological data. For example, lived and communal experiences are essential in the Arab world; thus, new and dynamic methods can be employed to ensure the authenticity of the data collected. This may necessitate new methods to capture high-quality, meaningful data, including natural language processes and computational techniques for Arabic language analysis and emerging qualitative methodological approaches like community engaged and participatory action research to optimize data collection and analysis to further develop Arab criminology.

Moreover, since there is very little access to social science data in the Arab world, it is fundamental that Arab governments and academic institutions establish methods of conduct, efficient collection processes, and transfer of data collected to create an atmosphere of accountability and transparency. The challenge to Arab criminologists will be localized within each national setting as they identify barriers to creating pragmatic solutions, including sociocultural questions that may impact how data is collected, viewed, incorporated, trusted, and ultimately integrated into the research process. Hence, it is important because even when Arab academics and researchers collect data, there is no centralized data base available in most of the Arab world, which limits its use for research and policy construction by other scholars.

Often the criminological data that is published and stored by state agencies is highly politicized and only descriptive relaying the number of criminal activities and arrests made with no contextual information and associated identifiers of the offenders or the victims. Ultimately, this severely limits the potential of the data collected, constrains the capacity of the Arab criminologists to conduct and write valuable research, and curtails the growth of Arab criminology. Furthermore, the limited access to data will restrict the capacity of Arab criminologists to capture or employ accurate criminological analysis.

The lack of access to social science–related data in the Arab world is often intentional and calculated as regimes restrict the type of data that can be collected to maintain control and shape the crime and crime control narrative in their respective contexts (Ouassini & Ouassini, 2020). It is essential for the data collected by Arab criminologists to be bound by ethical principles while ensuring that the studied communities are protected as previously established data in the Arab world is a tool that can be used by repressive regimes to undermine, imprison, and attack individuals, organizations, and civil society. The responsibility of Arab criminologists to safeguard their subjects is of utmost importance, and protocols adapted from the Northern models can be tremendously beneficial for Arab academics.

The Future of Arab Criminology

The future of Arab criminology will have many hurdles as the discipline defines its porous boundaries and engages in a region that is in politically uncertain terrain. However, the deep tradition of the social sciences in the Arab world provides the Arab criminologist a pathway from which Arab criminology can mobilize, institutionalize, and become mainstreamed in Arab academic institutions. At the outset, this would entail Arab criminologists working within and outside the Arab world to utilize a transdisciplinary approach as a framework to build the discipline in Arab universities. The framework must include faculty and specialists in all the sciences and humanities to develop a cadre of individuals who write and conduct research on criminology in the Arab world. In time, the subdiscipline of Arab criminology will evolve, expand, and constrict as it develops its institutions, scholars, journals, and sound scientific research.

The emerging Arab criminological tradition will operate in between and through Northern, Southern, and decolonial criminologies to work with Arab scholars and Arabists in the North to collaborate and aid in developing the subdiscipline. Indeed, this is important as the rigorous social scientific work conducted on the Arab world has primarily been done by Arab scholars residing in the North as the "works produced in the Arab world are poor relative to those produced by Arab intellectuals who reside, write, and publish in foreign languages abroad" (Abdul-Jabar, 2014, p. 503). This is evidenced by the fact that "the number of nationals of an Arab country among scientists abroad can be larger than the number of researchers in their home countries" (Hanafi & Arvanitis, 2014, p. 729). Moreover, the leading criminological studies on crime and criminal justice in the Arab world have been produced primarily from reports published by policy institutes, civil society organizations, and non-governmental organizations including the United Nations, Human Rights Watch, and Arab-world based think tanks and policy institutes.

In addition, Badry and Willoughby (2016) argue that the recent emergence of Western-based universities in the Arab world, namely, in the Arab Gulf, has been transformative in creating a slightly more open academic climate for debate (61). In addition, this policy shift in the Arab Gulf has led to the adoption of Western accreditation systems (Badry & Willoughby, 2016, p. 137) and institutions to build research capacity (McGlennon, 2006) and provides opportunities and access to local scholars to understand and engage Northern research. Hanafi and Arvanitis (2014) further maintain that a critical component of social scientific research in the Arab world is the "tradition of public debate." This public or applied criminology of sorts resorts to the publications of research and write-ups in local publications and newspapers as opposed to formal academic journals, which, in the case of criminology, are almost always English and French (Hanafi & Arvanitis, 2014, p. 736). Certainly, Arab criminology must formally integrate this medium of publications to guarantee that the discipline does not decenter the established criminological scholarship as "many research pieces are local, empirical, and remain in the form of reports rarely diffused" (Hanafi & Arvanitis, 2014, p. 729). Likewise, it ensures that these local scholars and specialists are integrated into the subdiscipline of Arab criminology.

Another critical development of Arab criminology is the establishment of criminology departments across universities in the Arab world. The lack of criminology programs, departments, and even courses in Arab universities is disconcerting; however, it also reveals the potential for Arab criminology as an academic discipline to emerge, grow, and prosper. This allows for the study of crime, criminality, and justice administration to emerge from the shadows of other disciplines in the Arab world, including sociology, criminal law, political science, and Islamic law. One of the few established criminal justice programs in the Arab world is the Naif Arab University for Security Sciences. As the academic arm of the Arab Interior Ministers Council (AIMC) representing all 22 Arab league states, it conducts academic research across the Arab world to "develop and strengthen cooperation and coordinate efforts between Arab countries in the field of internal security and combating crime" (Naif Arab University, 2022) with the intended goal of producing a cadre of next-generation scholars in the field of criminology and criminal justice in leadership positions in Arab security institutions across the Arab world. The Naif Arab University is currently the leading criminal justice-based university in the Arab world, with Arab-based criminal justice scholars and faculty representing several Arab nations. The institution is keen to be a leading criminal justice research center to pioneer the development of Arab criminology, coalescing the foremost criminologists and criminal justice practitioners across the Arab world.

While the structure of Naif Arab University, like many universities across the Arab world, is directly tied to the Arab League and its 22 member states, it is vital to recognize the potential impact and value of this university institution in the development of Arab criminology. The university leadership has established three journals in the Arabic language, a policy institute, a university press, and an innovation lab focused on criminal justice research. The academic journals include the *Arab Journal for Security Studies*, the *Journal of Information Security and Cybercrime Research*, and the *Arab Journal of Forensic Sciences and Forensic Medicine*. A review of the articles published reveals that nearly all of the studies were conducted by Arab social scientists and criminologists within and about the Arab world and were mainly engaging with and integrating Northern theories and models. The importation of Northern criminological theories in their analysis was descriptive and primarily focused on offenders. Nevertheless, these profound institutional developments are vital processes that are shaping the emergence and establishment of Arab criminology.

The level of engagement from Arab states in the AIMC and the Naif Arab University reveals that the support for developing Arab criminology is increasingly becoming widespread and no longer present only in the periphery in a few academic institutions in Saudi Arabia, Jordan, Lebanon, and Morocco or the Western universities in the Arab world whose criminal justice programs and courses are modeled on American and European curriculum and programming. The establishment of Naif Arab University and other criminal justice programs has already enabled the growth and expansion of academic research, conferences, academic societies, and organizations and the development of peer-reviewed journals, policy institutes, and train graduates to pursue evidence-based approaches and policies in their respective criminal justice systems. Arguably, the emerging discipline will produce better crime control models; increase trust, communication, and collaboration between criminal justice actors, academia, and civil society; and produce more vigorous and accurate data infrastructure and research.

Finally, the academic endeavor to institutionalize Arab criminology should not seek to do away with the existing public/applied criminology and its approaches in engaging Arab society. These alternative forms of research dissemination conducted and posted online or active scholarly engagement with newspapers, social media, and state media will only enhance and legitimize the standing of criminology in the Arab world. These methods and established normative tools must be supported to ensure that criminologists continue to actively engage in the public sphere. Ultimately, this will also offer Northern and Southern criminologists' new paradigmatic approaches that can be employed and benefit Northern and Southern criminology.

Conclusion

As Arab criminology expands and makes its way across the Arab transnational chain, it is of utmost importance that Arab criminology and criminologists are reflexive in their standpoints with Northern, Southern, and decolonial approaches. The capacity to transport, rework, and develop (Liu, 2017) the conceptual, methodological, and theoretical orientations of Arab criminology will depend on several factors. Arab criminology must centralize a transdisciplinary approach to support existing research and resources to establish academic departments and research centers in Western and local universities in the Arab world. Furthermore, attention needs to be focused on the development of a transparent data infrastructure at the university and government levels, the establishment of Arab criminology conferences, think tanks and policy institutes, and rigorous peer-reviewed academic journals across the Arab world. These developments would provide a medium for the exchange of information and data to advance the subdiscipline of Arab criminology, create new North–South engagements that can contribute new theoretical and methodological approaches in criminology and criminal justice studies, and challenge orientalist paradigms and Islamophobic tropes that continue to define and shape research and policy on the Arab world.

References

Abdul-Jabar, F. (2014). Reflections on Arabs and sociology: insights into sociological schools of thought in the Arab World–challenges and issues. *Contemporary Arab Affairs*, 7(4), 499–509.

Alibeli, M., Kopera-Frye, K., Professor, P., & Biedenharm, J. (2011). Tribal law and restoring peace in society: The case of 'Al-jala'in Jordan. *International Journal of Business and Social Science*. https://www.researchgate.net/profile/Madalla-Alibeli/publication/228971574_Tribal_Law_and_Restoring_Peace_ in_Society_The_Case_of_'Al-jala'in_Jordan/links/56701cc708ae5252e6f1d1c0/Tribal-Law-and-Restoring-Peace-in-Society-The-Case-of-Al-jalain-Jordan.pdf

Alotaibi, N. I., Evans, A. J., Heppenstall, A. J., & Malleson, N. S. (2019). How well does Western environmental theory explain crime in the Arabian context? The case study of Riyadh, Saudi Arabia. *International Criminal Justice Review*, 29(1), 5–32.

Badry, F., & Willoughby, J. (2016). *Higher education revolutions in the Gulf: Globalization and institutional viability (Routledge advances in Middle East and Islamic studies)* (1st ed.). Routledge.

Bagader, A. (1997). The state of Arab sociology as seen by an Arab sociologist. *Questions from Arab Societies*, 62–72. www.isasociology.org/uploads/files/Chapter%203%286%29.pdf

Bennett, R. R., & Lynch, J. P. (1996). Towards a Caribbean criminology: Prospects and problems. *Caribbean Journal of Criminology & Social Psychology*, 1(1), 8–37.

Bobseine, H. (2019). *Tribal justice in a Fragile Iraq*. The Century Foundation, 1–24.

Carrington, K., Hogg, R., & Sozzo, M. (2016). Southern criminology. *British Journal of Criminology*, 56(1), 1–20. https://doi.org/10.1093/bjc/azv083

Hanafi, S., & Arvanitis, R. (2014). The marginalization of the Arab language in social science: Structural constraints and dependency by choice. *Current Sociology*, 62(5), 723–742. https://doi.org/10.1177/0011392114531504

Hanafi, S., & Arvanitis, R. (2016). *Knowledge production in the Arab world: The impossible promise (Routledge advances in Middle East and Islamic studies)* (1st ed.). Routledge.

Ibrahim, S. E. (1997). Cross-eyed sociology in Egypt and the Arab world. *Contemporary Sociology*, 26(5), 547. https://doi.org/10.2307/2655614

Jones, H. (1981). *Crime, race and, and culture*. Wiley.

Liu, J. (2017). The Asian criminological paradigm and how it links global north and south: Combining an extended conceptual toolbox from the north with innovative Asian contexts. *International Journal for Crime, Justice and Social Democracy*, 6(1), 73–87. https://doi.org/10.5204/ijcjsd.v6i1.385

McGlennon, D. (2006). *Building research capacity in the gulf cooperation council countries: Strategy, funding and engagement*. http://portal.unesco.org/pv_obj_cache/pv_obj_id_02DCDD543BD8930F0C0A68F80DC77E24AAB70100/filename/McGlennon- EN.pdf.

Mesbahi, N. (2018). The victimization of the "Muslim woman": The case of Amina Filali, Morocco. *Journal of International Women's Studies*, 19(3), 49–59.

Moosavi, L. (2019). A friendly critique of "Asian criminology" and "Southern criminology". *The British Journal of Criminology*, 59(2), 257–275.

Naif Arab University. (2022). https://nauss.edu.sa/en-us/about-nauss/Pages/arab-Interior-ministers.aspx

Ouassini, A. (2019). We are all Amina Filali: Social media, civil society, and rape legislation reform in Morocco. *Women & Criminal Justice*, 31(1), 77–82.

Ouassini, N., & Ouassini, A. (2019). Criminology in the Arab World: Misconceptions, nuances and future prospects. *The British Journal of Criminology*, 60(3), 519–536. https://doi.org/10.1093/bjc/azz067

Ouassini, N., & Ouassini, A. (2020). Criminology in the Arab world: Misconceptions, nuances and future prospects. *The British Journal of Criminology*, *60*(3), 519–536.

Sabagh, G., & Ghazalla, I. (1986). Arab sociology today: A view from within. *Annual Review of Sociology*, *12*(1), 373–399. https://doi.org/10.1146/annurev.so.12.080186.002105

Wardak, A. (2019). Afghanistan: State and non – state-oriented criminal justice systems. In K. Jaishankar (Ed.), *Routledge handbook of South Asian criminology*. Routledge.

Index

Abbasids 36–37
Abu Ghraib scandal 10, 40, 44
Afghanistan 37; Afghan War 40, 71; Taliban takeover 27; U.S. invasion of 69; U.S. War on Terror 9
Al Qaeda 3, 40; September 11 attacks from 71, 72
Arab Convention for the Suppression of Terrorism 69, 71, 75
Arab criminology: challenges of 85–86; conceptualization of 11; data for 86–88; development of 81–83; establishing parameters of 81–83; framing 4–10; future of 88–91; future of race and crime 54–55; gender and policing 59–60; history of 38–39; international collaboration 75–77; Islamic law and 19–20, 27–29; media and 43–44; Northern, Southern and decolonial traditions 83–85; race and 51–54; subfield of 12; viability of 87
Arab identity 33–34; categories of 36; linguistic conceptualization 34–35; parameters of 11–12
Arab Interior Ministers Council (AIMC) 76, 77, 89, 90
Arab League 12, 13, 40, 75; alliance of 34; combatting transnational crime 75–77; definition 33–34; founding of 33, 45; pan-Arab movement and 39–40; terrorism definition 69
Arab nationalism 11, 12, 34, 36–38, 45
Arab Revolt 37, 38
Arab Spring 1, 2, 4, 5, 40, 41, 72; aftermath of 74; decade after 34; media and 43; pre- and post- 2

Arab women, as victims and offenders of crime 57–59
Arab World: Arab women as victims and offenders of crime 57–59; collective history of 33, 35–39; culture 33, 42–44; future of gender and crime in 60–61; future of race and crime in 54–55; gender and crime in 55–56; gender and policing 59–60; gender-based violence (GBV) in 56–57; Islamic law and 12–13; political systems 39–42; race and crime in 49–51
Asian criminology 5, 7
authoritarianism 28, 42, 84; Arab Spring and 72; Arab states 34, 41, 45, 85–86; digital 43; regime of Ben Ali 1

Ba'athism 26; Ba'ath Party 11; ideology 12
Baghdadi, Abu Bakr al- 3, 71
bin Laden, Osama 40, 71
Black Lives Matter 3, 54
Bush administration, invasion of Iraq 9–10, 40

Cold War 26, 70, 71
colonialism, legal importation and 25–27
colonization 6, 7, 20, 39, 84; European 11, 24, 51, 83; French 53; propagandized 25
communism 9, 71
COVID-19 pandemic: onset 3; protocols 60
crime: Arab women as victims and offenders 57–59; future of, in Arab

world 54–55; future of gender and, in Arab world 60–61; gender and, in Arab world 55–56; race and, in Arab world 49–51

criminology: in Arab world 81; decolonization of 5–8; factors of 4; framing Arab 4–10; Global North and Global South 5–8; rapid progression 3–4; *see also* Arab criminology

Crusades 19, 37, 69

culture: Arab world 33, 42–44; language and 34

decolonial criminology 88; Arab criminology as subdiscipline 83–85, 91

decolonization 39, 84; criminology 6–8, 10, 12

domestic violence 54, 55, 58

drug trafficking 13, 58, 68–69; reducing 76; transnational crime 72–73, 75

Egypt: national identity 52–53; United Arab Republic 12

epistemicide 6, 9

Facebook 43; group "We are all Khaled Saeed", 2

female offenders: crime in Arab world 56–57; *see also* gender

Gaza Strip, occupation of 53, 54

gender: Arab women as victims and offenders of crime 57–59; crime and in Arab world 55–56; future of crime and in Arab world 60–61; policing and 59–60; violence in Arab world 56–57

globalization 44, 84

Global North 5–6, 8, 19, 39, 56, 59

Global South 6, 8, 19, 59

"green scare" 9, 27

hawala, money transfers 75–76

history, Arab world 33, 35–39

human trafficking/smuggling 13, 68; transnational crime 74–75

Iberian Reconquista 19, 37

ideologies: Arab nationalism 45; Arab organizations 69, 71; Orientalist 8;

Ba'athist 12; German nationalist 34; political 9, 11, 39; racial 50–52

immigration, *kafala* system 74–75

Indigenous people 6, 7, 9; Arab criminology 84; religion 36; scholars researching women and crime 56

Iranian Revolution 27, 40, 71

Iraq 3, 23, 33, 70, 76; drugs 73; human smuggling 75; identity 82; Iraq War 27, 71; sectarianism 41; U.S. invasion of 9–10, 40, 42, 44, 69, 72, 74; Yazidi women of 59

Islam: emergence of 36; indigenous religion of Arabs 36

Islamic law: Arab criminology and 19–20, 27–29; Arab world and 12–13; colonialism and legal importation 25–27; *fiqh* 20, 21, 24, 26, 27–29; fundamental concepts of 20; *hadd/hudad* 20, 23–24, 28; legal system 20–24; *qadis* 25, 26; *qisas* 20, 23, 24, 28; *shari'a* 20, 21–22, 26, 27–29; *ta'zir* 20, 23–24, 28

Islamic State of Iraq and Syria (ISIS) 3, 27, 59

Islamophobia 9, 27, 29

kafala system: Arab Gulf 54; Arab women as offenders 58; human smuggling 74–75; immigration 74–75

Kurdish communities 35, 53

Lewis, Bernard 9, 10

Libya 2, 39, 70; Arab League 33, 34, 76; conflict in 72, 74; destruction of 71; drug trafficking 73; Federation of Arab Republics 12; political conditions 40–41; slavery in post-Qaddafi 53

media, Arab culture and 42–44

MENA (Middle East and North Africa) region 5, 9, 10; drug trafficking 73; race and Arab criminology 51–52

Mohammed, Prophet 21, 28, 82; mission 36

Nahda (Renaissance) Movement 33–34, 36

Naif Arab University 89–90

Nasser, Jamal Abdel 11–12, 39–40, 42, 70
neo-liberalism 43, 84
Northern criminology 13, 88; Arab criminology as subdiscipline 83–85, 91; data infrastructure 86; perspective of 6; theories of 81–83

Orientalism 9, 10, 19, 27, 29; ideology 8–9
Ottomans 11, 22, 25, 37

pan-Arabism 12, 43, 70; Arab nationalism and 11; failures of 40; Nasser and 39, 42; resilience of 34
police violence 53, 54
politics: Arab systems 38–42; Arab world 33

Quran 21, 23, 24, 36

race: Arab criminology and 51–54; crime and, in Arab world 49–51; future of, in Arab world 54–55
Regeni, Giulio, murder of 41–42
Regional Program for the Arab States to Prevent and Combat Crime Terrorism, and Health 75, 76

Said, Edward 8, 10, 25
September 11, terrorism 69, 71, 72
sexual assault, policing and 59–60
Shi'a population 23, 53, 54
slavery 6, 44, 55; anti-Black racism and 52; legalized 54; Libya 41, 53, 74; sexual 58
smuggling *see* human trafficking/smuggling
social media 2, 40, 43, 91
Somalia 33; conflict in 74, 85; drone attacks 27; drug trafficking 73
Southern criminology 8, 13, 88; approach 10; Arab criminology as subdiscipline 83–85, 91; perspective of 5, 6; theories of 81–83
Sunnah 21, 22, 23
Sykes-Picot Agreement 37–38
Syria 2, 3, 36; Arab League 33, 34; Assad's 12; conflict 72, 74, 85;
destruction of 71; drone attacks 27; drug trade 73; human smuggling 75; political conditions 40; race and 52; United Arab Republic 12; Yazidi women and 59

terrorism 9, 13; definition 69; September 11 69, 71, 72; transnational crime 69–72
trafficking *see* human trafficking/smuggling
transnational crime: Arab and international collaboration 75–77; definition by U.N. 68; drug trafficking 72–73; human trafficking 74–75; terrorism 69–72

Umayyad dynasty 36–37
United Nations Office of Drugs and Crime (UNODC) 77; Regional Program for the Arab states 13, 76, 77

violence 2, 6, 8–10, 44; in Algeria 38; in Darfur 52; domestic 54, 55, 58; gender-based (GBV) 56–57, 59; gendered 55; government using 44; in Lebanon 51; organized 25; police 53; political 28, 40, 69; renouncing 72; revolutionary change and 40; state-led 53–54, 55, 70; tribal 83

War on Terror 3, 5, 9, 27, 40, 42, 69, 71, 74
Weld El 15, 44
West Bank 53, 54

Yemen 23, 37, 40, 70; Al Qaeda 71; Arab League 33; conflict in 72, 74; destruction of 71; drone attacks 27; drug trafficking 73; humanitarian crisis 41; human rights 2; human trafficking 74; political conditions 40; race in 53; tribal communities 82–83; United Arab Republic 12; Zaydis in 23

Zarqawi, Abu Musab al- 3, 71
Zawahiri, Ayman al- 3, 71
Zionism 37–38

Printed in the United States
by Baker & Taylor Publisher Services